Hey, Bug Doctor!

Hey, Bug Doctor!

The Scoop on Insects in Georgia's Homes and Gardens

JIM HOWELL

Jon Davies, Photo Editor

The University of Georgia Press
Athens and London

© 2006 by the University of Georgia Press
Athens, Georgia 30602
All rights reserved
Designed by Walton Harris
Set in 10/15 Scala
Printed and bound by C & C Offset Printing, Inc.
The paper in this book meets the guidelines for
permanence and durability of the Committee on
Production Guidelines for Book Longevity of the
Council on Library Resources.

Printed in China
10 09 08 07 06 P 5 4 3 2 1

Library of Congress Cataloging-in-Publication Data

Howell, Jim, 1943–
Hey, bug doctor! : the scoop on insects in Georgia's homes
and gardens / Jim Howell ; Jon Davies, photo editor.
    p.   cm.
Includes index.
ISBN-13: 978-0-8203-2804-1 (pbk. : alk. paper)
ISBN-10: 0-8203-2804-9 (pbk. : alk. paper)
1. Insects—Georgia. 2. Insect pests—Georgia. I. Title.
QL475.G4H69 2006
595.709758—dc22   2005035685

British Library Cataloging-in-Publication Data available

Contents

Acknowledgments   *ix*

Introduction   *1*

LAWN AND GARDEN INSECTS

Dragonflies and Damselflies: Beautiful Colors for Your Fall Garden   *12*

Doodlebugs: Part of Rural Americana   *15*

Praying Mantises: Always Good to See in the Garden   *18*

Maggots: Our Friends (Sometimes)   *21*

Cicada Killers: More Bluff than Bite   *24*

Fire Ants: A Double Whammy of Pain   *27*

Carpenter Ants: Not the Home Remodelers You Want   *31*

Honey Bees: Where Have They Gone?   *34*

Bumble Bees: Unappreciated Pollinators   *37*

Carpenter Bees: Grab Your Broom Handle, Junior — They're Back   *40*

Hornets: Fierce, Feisty, and Worthy of Respect   *43*

Yellowjackets: Unwelcome Summer Guests   *46*

Mud Daubers: Industrious Masons   *49*

Paper Wasps: Not on the Front Porch, Please!   *52*

Ladybugs: Beneficial in the Garden, Pests in the House   *56*

Aphids: If Leaves Have Honeydew, It Must Be Summer   *59*

Bagworms: Homegrown Christmas Ornaments?   *63*

Tent Caterpillars: "Cotton Candy" in Your Cherry Trees?   *65*

Fall Webworms: Another Unsightly Nuisance   68

Yellow-necked Caterpillars: What Happened to My Shade?   70

Hickory Horned Devils: Dragons in the Trees   73

Luna Moths: Charming Guests in Your Garden   75

Boxelder Bugs: Big Nuisance Inside, Little Threat Outside   77

Euonymus Scales: Measles Mean a Big Problem   80

Hornworms: Attack of the Tomato Killers   83

Vine Borers and Pickleworms: Watch for Them in Summer Squash   86

Lace Bugs: Far from Fragile   89

Spittlebugs: Frothy Masses in Your Grasses?   91

Wheel Bugs: Modern-Day Garden Dinosaurs   93

Whiteflies: Are the Gardenias Smoking?   96

White Grubs: Don't They Make Your Green Lawn Brown   99

Fireflies: Fairy Lanterns in the Backyard   102

Asian Tiger Mosquitoes: Backyard Nuisance and Health Concern   105

Lubber Grasshoppers: Usually Harmless Giants   108

Dog-day Cicadas: The Original Summer Buzz   111

Relatives

Spider Mites: Nasty in Hot, Dry Weather   116

Golden Garden Spiders: Welcome This Web Weaver to Feast
in Your Garden   119

Millipedes and Centipedes: Mainly Just a Nuisance   122

Chiggers: Ooooohhh, Those Itchy Redbugs!   125

Ticks: Don't Get "Ticked" with Warm Spring Weather   128

HOUSEHOLD INSECTS

Bedbugs and Batbugs: Tiny Bedroom Vampires *132*

Moth Flies: Unwanted Guests in Your Drains *135*

Fruit Flies: Drunk on Their Own Success *138*

Cluster Flies: They Only Seem like a Serious Problem *141*

Cockroaches: Will They Outlast Us All? *144*

German Cockroaches: Small Insects, Big Problems *147*

Oriental Cockroaches: Nasty Nuisances *150*

Booklice: Tiny Bibliophiles *153*

Carpet Beetles: Another Personal Horror Movie *155*

Indian Meal Moths: You'll Need More than a Fly Swatter
to Get Rid of Them! *158*

Cigarette Beetles: More than Just a Tobacco Pest *161*

Saw-toothed Grain Beetles: Big Problem in a Small Package *164*

Clothes Moths: They Can Turn Your Riches to Rags *166*

Fleas: If Thou Hast an Indoor Pet, Thou Shalt Have Them *169*

Head Lice: The Cooties Are Coming! *173*

Termites: Your Home Is Their Sunday Buffet *176*

Camel Crickets: Humpbacked Moisture Lovers *181*

Earwigs: Horror Movie Monsters *184*

Silverfish and Firebrats: No Laughing Matter *187*

Relatives

Daddy-longlegs: Alien Invaders? *192*

Dust Mites: Gesundheit! *195*

Common House Spiders: Messy but Harmless   *198*

Black Widows and Brown Recluses: Are They Really
Husband Killers and Loners?   *201*

Sowbugs and Pillbugs: Invasion of the Bantam Armadillos!   *205*

Photo Credits   *209*

Index   *213*

Acknowledgments

There are countless people to whom I am thankful and without whose assistance and encouragement this book would not have been possible. First, I'd like to thank my grandfather, the late James Leonard Reynolds, whose guidance and explanations of the natural world around us inspired me during my childhood and throughout my life. My mother and stepfather, Margaret and Thomas Moore, have also been tremendous influences in my life; I owe them immeasurable gratitude. I also want to thank my wife, Estelle, for her suggestions and critiques of my columns prior to submission. And I'd like to thank my three beautiful daughters, Dana, Meg, and Jamie. Their interest in and experiences with the tiny creatures featured in this book during their childhoods still warm me with some very special memories.

Thanks are also due to all the readers of my column in the *Atlanta Journal and Constitution* for their questions and suggestions and for their continuing support. Since the column's inception back in 2001, the people of Atlanta and surrounding areas have received my offerings with enthusiasm and appreciation; their suggestions and comments have helped me as much as I have helped them.

I am also indebted to the numerous extension entomologists around the country whose general information on insects has been a large asset for me in both my columns and in this book.

And finally, I thank the editors at the University of Georgia Press: Nicole Mitchell, Christa Frangiamore, and Nancy Grayson, who suggested that such a book might be possible. To Christa Frangiamore I owe a special debt of gratitude. Her gentle but insistent prodding during the formulation of this work was greatly appreciated—and needed.

Introduction

Earth is populated by millions of species of insects, which affect our lives in myriad ways. Since the beginning of recorded history they have been both blessing and curse to humankind. We count them among our arch-enemies *and* our allies. Though pest species make up a very small percentage of the total, they make themselves very visible to us in the enormity of their destruction. They cause millions of dollars in damage each year to our agricultural crops, our ornamental plants, our clothing, our homes, and even our own bodies. Among the world's most important disease vectors, insects are responsible for millions of human deaths each year through the transmission of malaria and other diseases. They are also responsible for direct attacks on our pets and livestock leading to irritation, loss of productivity, and even death.

On the positive side, insects are the primary pollinators of our crops. They help us control pest species, they provide food for our wildlife, and they produce things that we use directly such as honey, beeswax, silk, and shellac. In some parts of the world they are an important source of protein. The Aborigines of Australia, for example, prize the witchety grub, a type of moth larva, and some African cultures eat locusts. Several aquatic species serve as excellent bioindicators of pollution in our streams. And we should not underestimate their aesthetic value. Iridescent dragonflies weaving patterns of light as they patrol lakes, tiger swallowtails drifting effortlessly above the garden, a ghostly luna moth flying through the dusk—these insect encounters and others add enormously to our lives.

I have been writing a column on insects for the *Atlanta Journal-Constitution* since the spring of 2001, much of which is the basis for this book. During that time I have received many wonderful letters from readers, not only commenting on the subjects I have covered but also mentioning other topics they would like to know more about. Their correspondence has given me a very good idea of what the general public finds interesting.

My e-mail address is hey_bug_doctor@hotmail.com. As the address implies, to many people I am the "bug doctor." They expect me to know the answer to virtually any question about any living animal that lacks a backbone. That is impossible, of course, but I do try to find answers to their insect questions and have written some of my favorite columns as a result.

When I taught general entomology at the University of Georgia, I often used *The Far Side* cartoons as illustrations of selected principles that I wanted my students to remember. Gary Larson has a unique ability to speak volumes with a single drawing and simple caption. He also has a biology background, and many of his entomological cartoons are factually accurate as well as amusing. I found that students usually remembered an idea that had been "tagged" with a *Far Side* cartoon. I use the same principle in my columns. Along with the necessary biological information for the various insects, I try to include a touch of humor. I also try to promote environmental responsibility. Although I usually end each column about a pest species with suggestions for its control, I encourage and prefer any control methodology that resists the use of pesticides. Of course, I also recognize that there are times when pesticides are the only reasonable alternative.

Not all insects are pests. There are many harmless species that enrich our lives simply by the grace and beauty of their existence. They are worth getting to know.

WHAT ARE INSECTS?

Insects are among the oldest and most successful life forms on Earth. Taxonomists — biologists who specialize in classifying animals and plants — have estimated that there are several million species of insects. Almost 75 percent of all animals are insects, as are about half of all described species of animals. The smallest species are not as big as some protozoa, and the largest are larger than our smallest mammals. This extreme variation in size allows insects to occupy a tremendous range of habitats in virtually every environmental condition, and to have lifestyles ranging from parasites to predators, scavengers, and phytophages (plant eaters).

As insects mature, they pass through several stages, or instars. Some insects, like grasshoppers and roaches, have a similar appearance from the time they leave the egg until they are adults. This type of development is called hemimetabolous, or gradual metamorphosis. Others, like the butterflies, beetles, and wasps, have larval (immature) stages that look very different from the adult forms. This form of development is called holometabolous, or complete metamorphosis.

Insects, like other living things, are classified within a rather complex hierarchy based on specific physical characteristics. All animals, including insects, belong to the kingdom Animalia. The kingdom has six primary subdivisions: phylum, class, order, family, genus, and species.

Taxonomists fall into one of two categories. They tend to be either "lumpers" or "splitters," and serious splitters often subdivide the six categories into "supra" and "sub" divisions (e.g., supraorder and subspecies). Taxonomists make their living by publishing scientific papers that move various critters into and out of these categories. I know this is true because I did it myself for about 30 years.

Insects are classified in the phylum Arthropoda along with crabs, lobsters, shrimp, spiders, ticks, mites, scorpions, pillbugs, centipedes, millipedes, and daddy-longlegs. The insects form the class Insecta (or Hexapoda if you are a bit more "new age"), which—depending on the authority you ask—includes anywhere from 25 to 35 orders. The spiders, ticks, and daddy-longlegs are in the class Arachnida, and so on.

Because this can be a bit confusing, let's take the honey bee from the very top of the chain to the bottom:

Kingdom Animalia
  Phylum Arthropoda
    Class Insecta
      Order Hymenoptera (the bees, wasps, and ants)
        Family Apidae
          Genus *Apis*
            Species *mellifera*

Each species account in this book includes the various pigeonholes into which the critter fits. *Warning*: taxonomists are often a disagreeable lot, and there are differences of opinion regarding these placements. If you want to have fun with this book, don't take these categories too seriously.

Insects can be separated from other arthropods on the basis of their anatomy. All insects have three distinct body regions: a head, a thorax, and an abdomen (evolutionary modifications make it hard to distinguish them in some cases). All have one pair of antennae and three pairs of legs. No other arthropod group has three pairs of legs.

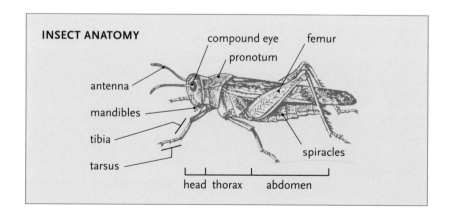

INSECT ANATOMY — compound eye, femur, pronotum, antenna, mandibles, tibia, tarsus, spiracles, head thorax abdomen

The class most commonly confused with insects is the Arachnida. Spiders, ticks, scorpions, daddy-longlegs, and mites are all arachnids. They have distinct characteristics of their own but are most easily distinguished from insects by the absence of antennae and the presence of four pairs of legs rather than three.

Centipedes and millipedes belong to their own classes within the Arthropoda (Chilopoda and Diplopoda, respectively). Centipedes have a long body that is divided into a head and a multisegmented trunk. Most segments *appear* to have a single pair of legs. The millipedes also have a pair of short antennae and a multisegmented trunk, but most segments *appear* to have two pairs of legs.

The pillbugs and sowbugs are classified in the subphylum Crustacea, and are actually more closely related to lobsters, crabs, and shrimp than to insects. They have seven pairs of legs and two pairs of antennae, only one of which is easily seen.

This book covers many of the most common insects found in Georgia homes and gardens. It is divided into two parts. The first part considers insects and their relatives found in and around lawns and gardens. The second part covers the house-infesting species: insects that eat the wood in our houses, the food in our kitchens, and the clothes in our closets (among other things). Some species fall into both categories.

Within each part are sections on individual groups or species. Each account includes the animal's scientific name, a description to help with identification, and a discussion of the animal's biology, impact on humans and the environment, and control measures. Boxes scattered throughout the text discuss topics of special interest (e.g., treating wasp stings, distinguishing between termites and ants). Because arachnids, centipedes, millipedes, and sowbugs are commonly encountered in homes and gardens — and occasionally offer problems to the homeowner and backyard gardener — I have included a few of them in this book as well. They are discussed in the "Relatives" section of each of the book's two parts.

PESTICIDES

A pesticide is a chemical substance used to prevent, repel, or destroy an insect or other animal that is causing harm. These come in various forms, including sprays, dusts, baits, powders, and aerosols. Whenever possible, other means of control should be tried before using pesticides. Sometimes, something as simple as "hand picking" can reduce the pest to acceptable numbers. Because pesticides are often necessary to gain the measure of control that we want, however, it behooves us to learn how to use them safely. Understanding their proper use is of the utmost importance to humans, to beneficial insects, and to the environment.

Perhaps the most important point when using pesticides is always to follow the directions on the label. It may be tempting to think that if 1 teaspoon per gallon is good, then 3 teaspoons will be better. That can be a serious mistake. Tripling the amount does not triple the pesticide's effectiveness, but it does triple the poison dose to everyone and everything exposed to it: your family and pets as well as the target insects. The manufacturers of the product have listed an effective dose on the label. Follow their recommendations for dose as well as the other safety precautions on the product's label. Overuse and misuse of pesticides can kill beneficial organisms and can contaminate our lakes and streams. Such misuse has resulted in the banning of some materials that, if used properly, might have served us effectively for many years.

Some chemicals take a longer time to break down than others do, and these tend to be the products that are more hazardous to the consumer. They may not be dangerous if handled according to the label instructions, but the risk increases greatly for someone who uses them carelessly. Shorter-lived chemicals are usually much safer to handle. Some of the safest are the pyrethrins and their derivatives.

An excellent discussion of the safe use of pesticides, written by Dr. Paul Guillebeau, an extension entomologist at the University of Georgia, College of Agriculture's Cooperative Extension Service, can be found in the 2005 *Pest Management Handbook* published by the Cooperative Extension Service (http://www.ent.uga.edu/pmh/).

GLOSSARY TO BIOLOGICAL TERMS

I have aimed to keep the text accessible to all readers, but nonbiologists will occasionally come across an unfamiliar term. So that you won't have to scramble for a dictionary while you're out in the yard, I have supplied some definitions for a few commonly used biological terms below.

cephalothorax	the fused head and thorax of Arachnida (spiders and their kin) and Crustacea
chelicerae	the mouthparts of spiders, corresponding to the mandibles of insects, from which the fangs extend
elytra (sing. *elytron*)	the hardened anterior wings of beetles and a few other insects that fold over and protect the posterior pair of wings
hemimetabolous	incomplete metamorphosis; a type of development in which the immature forms closely resemble the adults
holometabolous	complete metamorphosis; a type of development in which the immature forms vary greatly from the adult forms (e.g., caterpillar and butterfly)
instar	the stage of a developing insect between molts

larva	the immature stage of an insect
metamorphosis	the process of changing body form as insects pass through the various immature stages to adulthood
nymph	an immature insect in which the developing form closely resembles the adult (e.g., grasshoppers, silverfish)
ootheca	the protective covering for a mass of eggs
predaceous	capturing and feeding on other organisms, usually animals
pronotum	the top, or dorsal, plate of the first thoracic segment in insects
pupation	transformation of the larva into the pupa—the quiescent last stage between immature and adult
saprophytic	feeding on decaying organic matter
setae	specialized thick, hairlike projections on an insect's body
spiracle	openings through which air enters the tracheae that serve as an insect's breathing mechanism
stabilimentum	the heavily reinforced area of a spider's web, usually located in or toward the center
tarsus	the distal, or terminal, segment of an arthropod's leg
tibia	the segment of the insect leg immediately preceding the tarsus, or foot
tracheae	the internal air tubes that carry air to various parts of an insect's body

This book does not cover all—or even most—of the insects Georgians are likely to see in their yards, gardens, and homes. And I have not tried to describe those that are included here in scientific detail. There are many wonderful sources of information on insects in libraries, in bookstores, and on the Internet. I hope that after reading this book you will think twice before smashing that bug skittering across the kitchen floor. And if you then go on to smash it, do it with the respect and admiration the bug deserves. We share this planet with insects, and, like it or not, we have to deal with them. Isn't it better to do that with appreciation and humor?

Lawn and Garden Insects

Dragonflies and Damselflies
Beautiful Colors for Your Fall Garden

My grandfather called them "snake doctors." My earliest memory of these colorful creatures is of a creek bank in middle Virginia where I was sitting with my grandparents. A black-winged damselfly lit on the end of my grandmother's fishing pole and Pa whispered to me: "Look, Jimmy! That snake doctor's tellin' me your granny's about to get a bite." Sure enough, within a few minutes the float on my grandmother's line was bobbing up and down, and soon she was pulling in a nice bream that my grandfather happily tethered to his stringer.

The dragonflies are an ancient group. The oldest fossils recognizable as dragonfly relatives are from Upper Carboniferous deposits in Bavaria that are 350 million years old. The group is divided into two categories: the damselflies, sometimes called "snake doctors" because it was once believed they could bring snakes back to life, and dragonflies, sometimes called "horse stingers" or "devil's darning needles" from the belief that they would sew together the lips of wicked children while they slept. Dragonflies are such strong fliers that collectors have been known to shoot them down with small-gauge shotgun shells loaded with sand!

SCIENTIFIC NAMES Order Odonata; Suborders Zygoptera and Anisoptera

IDENTIFICATION Damselflies are usually smaller and more slender than dragonflies, and fly with a weak, fluttering flight. Their fore and hind wings are similar in shape and are tented over the body when at rest. Dragonflies are more robust. Their fore and hind wings are different in shape and are often held away from the body at an angle of about 180 degrees when at rest. Some dragonflies have a wingspan of several inches. With their wings

Dragonflies are among our most colorful insects.

and bodies adorned with various shades of black, red, blue, and green, the odonates are among the most colorful of our garden insects.

BIOLOGY All damselflies deposit their eggs into aquatic plant material either above or below the water's surface. Some dragonfly species do this as well; others lay their eggs directly in the water or in mud at the water's edge. The larvae live underwater and breathe through gills. All are voracious predators that feed on a variety of aquatic life, including fish spawn, tadpoles, and immature insects. They in turn are fed upon by fish, frogs, and some waterfowl. After the last larval instar, the newly emerged adults leave their aquatic environs and spend several days to several weeks away from water. During this time they disperse to other locations, become sexually mature, and take on their full adult coloration. They return to streams and ponds to mate.

IMPACT Damselfly and dragonfly larvae are a valuable food source for fish and other aquatic life, including some diving ducks. The adults are eaten by birds. They are completely harmless to humans. Those of us fortunate enough to have them in our gardens have a source of spectacular beauty. Dragonfly populations can be enhanced by encouraging and developing small ponds and lakes with surrounding vegetation.

Dragonflies are often found around water and are powerful fliers.

Doodlebugs
Part of Rural Americana

The sandy pits made by ant lion larvae are among our most vivid childhood memories. When I was about 6 years old, my grandfather used to quote this charm while lightly dragging a stick along the edges of an ant lion's home:

Ant lion larvae have powerful jaws.

> Doodlebug, doodlebug,
> Come out of your hole;
> Your house is on fire,
> And your children will burn.

It was my first exposure to these fascinating creatures. "Doodlebugs" have even carved out a niche in popular literature. Mark Twain clearly refers to memories of his youth in the following excerpt from *Tom Sawyer*:

> [Tom] laid himself down and put his mouth close to this depression and called—"Doodle-bug, doodle-bug, tell me what I want to know! Doodle-bug, doodle-bug, tell me what I want to know!" The sand began to work, and presently a small black bug appeared for a second and then darted under again in a fright. "He dasn't tell! So it was a witch that done it. I just knowed it."

Ant lion folklore dates back to the early days of American history and usually includes a charm or chant like those used by Tom Sawyer and my

Ant lion adults are weak fliers and resemble lacewings.

grandfather. Charles Duke, Apollo 16 astronaut, compared the lunar craters to ant lion pits and even recited part of a "charm" during his conversations from the moon: "Doodlebug, doodlebug, are you at home?" A larva big enough to make those craters would have easily eaten all the astronauts, and their tiny craft as well!

SCIENTIFIC NAMES Order Neuroptera; Family Myrmeleontidae

IDENTIFICATION Ant lion adults are fragile winged creatures that roughly resemble damselflies but are much weaker flyers. They are easily distinguished from damselflies by their clubbed antennae and different wing venation. The grayish body of the adults is usually about 1 ½ inches long.

Though fairly common, they are rarely seen because they are usually active late in the evening. Fully developed larvae are about as long as a human fingernail, a little more than ½ inch, with very long jaws that are much longer than the head.

BIOLOGY Ant lions are closely related to lacewings, but differ in that the adults are not predaceous. Adults are active in spring and summer. They lay eggs in soft, dry soil, often in sand. After the eggs hatch, the larvae dig pits — inverted cones — in loose soil and wait in ambush at the bottom, buried just beneath the sand. Clusters of cone-shaped pits can often be found in sheltered sandy spots such as dry, shady river banks and other wooded areas, in flower beds, and in the dry soil under eaves and other buildings elevated by piers or cinder blocks. An ant or other small insect that slips into the pit cannot extricate itself because the loose dirt on the sloping sides carries it to the bottom. The ant lion lying in wait below further hinders the struggling insect by tossing loose pieces of sand or grit at it. When the victim reaches the bottom, the ant lion grabs it with its huge jaws and literally sucks the fluids out of it.

IMPACT Ant lion larvae are voracious predators of ants, and as such are considered beneficial. Having a doodlebug near the house both reduces ant numbers and brings back happy memories. Those of us who are fortunate enough to see an adult ant lion in our garden should consider ourselves blessed.

Praying Mantises
Always Good to See in the Garden

The mantises, with their lightning-quick reflexes, are among the most efficient predators of all the insects. Some of the larger mantises have even been known to capture small birds. The common name, praying mantis, is derived from a Greek word meaning "diviner" or "prophet," and it conjures vivid images of the insect that carries it. My grandfather first introduced me to this large green predator, which he welcomed to his garden. "He always prays before he eats," my grandfather said, "and then he protects our garden from pests."

Many myths and exaggerated truths swirl about the praying mantis. In Europe, people once believed that a lost person who came across a mantis could find the way home by traveling in the direction the mantis was facing. The Arabs believed that mantids always faced Mecca, and some Africans even attributed to them the power to restore life. The most popular story holds that the female always eats the head of the male during mating. Though this is not always the case, it does occur with regularity, and it brings an entirely new perspective to the expression "losing one's head over a woman."

While I was a graduate student at Virginia Tech, I once shared my screened porch with five large orb-weaving spiders. A large mantis moved in one evening and over the next few days methodically captured each spider, snatching them from their webs and consuming them with relish.

SCIENTIFIC NAMES Order Mantoidea; Family Mantidae; *Mantis* sp.; Carolina mantid: *Stagmomantis carolina* (Johannson); Chinese mantid: *Tenodera aridifolia sinensis* Saussure

Mantids are efficient predators and are very beneficial in our gardens.

IDENTIFICATION Two mantid species are common in Georgia: the Carolina mantid and the Chinese mantid. The Carolina mantid is about 3–4 inches long and is more brownish than the Chinese mantid. The latter is larger, about 5–6 inches long, and more greenish in color. Mantids have a triangular head that moves freely on an elongate "neck," giving them the ability to look behind them without moving the body—an incredible advantage over prey. The front legs are modified into conspicuous grasping devices that shoot out to capture and hold prey. The lower portion of the tibia has very sharp spines that impale the victim and press it against the foreleg like a knife blade into its handle. It is this feature that presents the distinctive "praying" position from which this insect gets its common name.

BIOLOGY Adult females lay eggs in a foam-covered inch-long cluster called an ootheca that is attached to twigs, plant stems, and other surfaces, where it hardens into a tan mass. The eggs overwinter in the brownish foam, and young mantids hatch in spring with the onset of warm weather. From the moment of hatching, mantids are efficient eating machines that feed on anything they can catch, including animals larger than themselves and their own siblings.

IMPACT Mantids do not bite humans, nor are they considered pests, except to the extent that they eat insects humans consider beneficial. Their positive influence is far greater than the negative. Many people collect mantid egg cases each fall, keep them in a protected outside spot, and then place them in their gardens the next spring. Their large size makes mantids excellent class projects, and children always seem fascinated to watch a praying mantis capture its prey.

Maggots
Our Friends (Sometimes)

An entomologist friend of mine once told me of an incident in which he was called to a very nice upper-middle-class home where maggots had been found crawling across the family room floor. He collected them and allowed the specimens to pupate, and the emerging flies were identified as blowflies, whose larvae feed on dead animal tissue. The appearance of these maggots in a house typically indicates that an animal (a bird, mouse, squirrel, or the like) has died within the walls or in the attic. In this case there was

Blowflies usually deposit live larvae rather than eggs.

no odor leading to an animal carcass and no indication that the creatures had been brought in from outside. Often, entomologists have to be amateur detectives to figure out why an insect is in a particular place in order to determine how to proceed with its removal.

In this case, the maggots were coming from the body of a duck that had fallen into the fireplace chimney and was resting on top of the vent. Because the air draft carried all the odor of decay upward, no smell was detected inside. By asking where the larvae were first seen and where they had been the most numerous, the entomologist systematically eliminated possibilities until he finally looked up the chimney.

SCIENTIFIC NAMES Order Diptera; Family Calliphoridae; Green bottle fly: *Phaenicia sericata* (Meigen); Blue bottle fly: *Calliphora vomitoria* (Linnaeus)

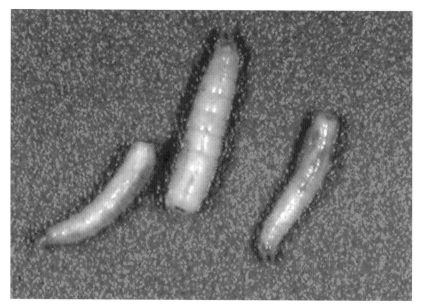

Maggots are usually a sign of decaying animal flesh.

IDENTIFICATION Several blowfly species are common in Georgia. Adults of most of these species have a characteristic color, varying from shiny blue to green to yellow, and are commonly called "bottle flies." The larvae are typical "maggots": tiny wriggling masses of flesh without legs or a well-defined head.

BIOLOGY Blowflies are attracted to the gases emitted from decaying bodies. They are very strong fliers and often find dead animals within minutes of death. On finding a decaying body, a blowfly will lay hundreds of eggs, and the larvae that hatch from them will feed on the carcass until no tissue is left. Blowflies are often found in homes in the winter, especially if homeowners have used a rodenticide to control mice or rats. Animals killed by these poisons often die within a wall space or an attic, and blowflies will be around to find them. They can also reproduce in manure when an animal carcass is not available.

IMPACT Blowflies are usually considered beneficial because they are nature's undertakers; they are very important in the decomposition of dead animals and in the recycling of these materials back into the environment. They are useful to law enforcement as well. The presence of adult blowflies on a body indicates a recent demise. The presence and age of larvae are also indicators of time of death. When they occur in homes, blowflies are a nuisance because of their constant loud buzzing, which some people confuse with the sounds made by wasps or bees. They are attracted to light and eventually end up at a window, where they bang against the windowpanes in their attempts to escape.

CONTROL Usually no control is necessary. Removal of the animal carcass will remove the flies. Space sprays and surface sprays containing pyrethrins can be used as a last resort.

Cicada Killers
More Bluff than Bite

I know you have seen them—flying fast and low over the ground, zooming around your flower beds and gardens like 2-inch fighter planes ready to strafe an enemy hiding among the flowers. These are cicada killers—solitary wasps that are far more menacing than they are harmful. When we were children, my cousins Vernon and Earl and I pretended they *were* warplanes and we were the antiaircraft fire. We'd load our slingshots with BBS and try to shoot the wasps out of the air as they glided past.

Several years ago I encountered a particularly aggressive male that was determined to defend the cup on the seventh green at the Griffin Country Club golf course. It was amusing to watch golfers putt out and then try to get the ball out of the cup while avoiding the dive-bombing wasp.

SCIENTIFIC NAMES Order Hymenoptera; Family Sphecidae; *Sphecius speciosus* (Drury)

IDENTIFICATION Cicada killers are very large solitary wasps about 1⅛ to 1¾ inches long. They have brownish wings and a very robust reddish black body with transverse yellow bands across both the thorax and the frontmost part of the abdomen.

BIOLOGY The female cicada killer spends most of her time up in the trees searching for cicadas. When she finds one, she paralyzes it with her sting. She then straddles the cicada, grasps it with her long legs, and "glides" down from the tree in the direction of her burrow. After hitting the ground, she will drag the cicada the rest of the way. Each female digs an individual nest 6–10 inches deep and about ½ inch wide, dislodging the soil with her

Cicada killer males are very territorial but cannot sting.

mouth and kicking it backward like a dog burying a bone. The entrance to each burrow is marked by a U-shaped mound of this dirt. The nests may be found in a variety of places but are most common in full sun where vegetation is sparse—like lawns, golf course sand traps, flower beds, window boxes, and so on. The female drags the paralyzed cicada down into the burrow and may add one or two more cicadas before depositing a single egg. She then seals the tunnel. The larva feeds on the cicada for about a week and a half, then becomes dormant for the winter. Adults live about 2 to 2 ½ months and are most active from mid-July to early September.

IMPACT These wasps are usually considered beneficial because they prey on cicadas, which are pests of our trees and shrubs. If possible they should be left alone. The females are not aggressive and will rarely sting unless provoked (grabbed, caught in clothing, and so on). The slightly smaller males cannot sting, but they aggressively defend their territory and have sent many screaming youngsters—and their parents—running for the back door!

CONTROL The best way to control cicada killers is through prevention. The cultivation of a healthy, lush lawn without bare spots in which the wasps can tunnel is the best first step. If insecticides are necessary, a material like carbaryl dust can be used if the infestation is widespread and covers a large area. Check with your county extension agent for additional pesticide options. If you do not want to use pesticides but still want to reduce populations, get an old tennis racquet and flail away. And for the purist who wants an even greater challenge—try a slingshot with BBs.

Fire Ants

A Double Whammy of Pain

Myth and misinformation surround these tiny creatures. Fire ants have been blamed for everything from the death of newborn calves to the destruction of expensive farming equipment. Though there is a whisper of truth behind some of these claims, most are blown far out of proportion. In the overall scheme of life, fire ants are very beneficial organisms. On the other hand, they can be a very serious nuisance to homeowners and farmers. Those who have had an unpleasant experience with them feel a cold shiver down the spine at the mention of their flaming moniker. An old farmer friend of mine says that fire ants never sting one at a time. Instead, they quietly crawl up inside your pants legs, then one will whistle and they all sting you at once.

A fire ant worker forages for food.

Fire ants defend their nest aggressively and in large numbers.

SCIENTIFIC NAMES Order Hymenoptera; Family Formicidae; *Solenopsis invicta* Buren; *Solenopsis* sp.

IDENTIFICATION At least three species of fire ants are found in Georgia. The imported red fire ant is by far the most aggressive and has displaced the other two over much of the South. Adult workers are reddish brown to black and about ⅛ inch to ¼ inch long. The mounds that mark their nests may be 1–2 feet high and have a very characteristic "crusty" exterior. The soil of other ant mounds will always have a loose texture. The mounds contain ants of various sizes, and they will collectively attack—in large numbers—anything that threatens the colony.

BIOLOGY In spring, summer, and fall—often after a rain—winged males and females leave the mound and mate in flight. After mating, they descend to the ground and shed their wings. Most of the young queens are killed by other foraging ants, but the survivors burrow into the soil and begin new colonies of their own, sometimes up to 10 miles from the original site. The size of the resulting mound is directly proportional to the population in the colony. Colonies at least 1 year old may contain more than 100,000 workers. Healthy mature colonies may contain up to 300,000 workers.

IMPACT Fire ants are omnivorous and very opportunistic in their search for food. They feed on plants and animals—dead or alive—and as a consequence often come into conflict with farmers and homeowners. When fire ants and humans occupy the same spot, confrontations are bound to result. The ants get their name from the fiery sensation caused by the venom in their sting. They also bite, and the result is a "double whammy" of pain and discomfort. The ants first grip the skin with their mandibles and then sting several times in a circular pattern around the site of the bite. Most stings result in a slightly swollen red area with a blister in the middle. Hypersensitive individuals, however, may suffer an anaphylactic reaction to fire ant stings. Anyone displaying distinct symptoms of wheezing, shortness of breath, hives, dizziness, weakness, or confusion following a fire ant sting should receive immediate medical attention.

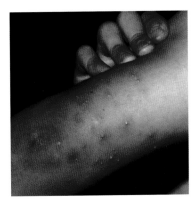

Fire ant stings

Because fire ant mounds are relatively hard and are substantial in size, they can cause damage to farming equipment. The ants occasionally attack unprotected newborn farm animals and have also been known to damage young plants, fruits, and berries. These are relatively rare occurrences, however, and fire ants are not generally considered to be of major economic importance to crops, livestock, or wildlife.

On a positive note, because fire ants are very good predators, they may act as biological control agents for our gardens. If they are in an area that is not often frequented by humans, they should be left alone.

CONTROL Several options are available for the control of ants in heavily populated areas.

1. Drenches. Mound drenches—pesticides diluted in water—are contact insecticides that must seep down through the mound and come in contact with the ants to be effective. For total destruction of the colony the queen must be reached, and she is often several feet beneath the surface. Drenches are used when the ant infestation must be removed immediately.

2. Baits. Around homes, baits are usually the method of choice if immediate removal is not imperative. Baits are a mixture of ant attractants and pesticides. The workers forage on these particles, take them into the mound, and feed them to the queen. This process may take several weeks to kill all the workers in the mound.

3. Broadcast applications. The distribution of bait over a relatively large area has the disadvantage of perhaps disrupting native ant populations as well. This method should be used only when high fire ant mound densities are present.

Carpenter Ants

Not the Home Remodelers You Want

Ants are well known for their work ethic. Such wordsmiths as Aesop, Ogden Nash, and Robert Frost have praised their industriousness. Even the Bible makes reference to their wisdom. In Proverbs 30:25, we are told: "The ants are a people not strong, yet they prepare their meat in the summer." And in Proverbs 6:6, we are admonished: "Go to the ant, thou sluggard; consider her ways and be wise." But in late spring and summer, when we are assailed by an endless ant armada, it's difficult to admire ants' assiduous behavior. One of the most bothersome species to invade our home is the carpenter ant. Though carpenter ants don't use hammers or saws or lay out their work with a chalk line, if undiscovered or left alone they can cause significant damage to the structure of a house.

Carpenter ants can cause significant structural damage to your house.

SCIENTIFIC NAMES Order Hymenoptera; Family Formicidae; *Camponotus* sp.

IDENTIFICATION Carpenter ants, which are among the largest ants in Georgia, include several species in the genus *Camponotus*. Like other ants, they are social insects, living in colonies with castes that perform different jobs. Workers come in several sizes, ranging from ¼ to ⁷⁄₁₆ inch in length, while the queen usually exceeds ½ inch. The black carpenter ant is one of the most common. It is primarily black, while the other species are reddish brown to yellow.

BIOLOGY Carpenter ants do not eat wood like their distant cousins the termites. Instead, they tunnel through it while building and expanding their nests. In their natural habitat they are found in tree stumps, dead trees, logs, and tree holes. Their preferred food is honeydew, a sugar compound secreted by certain plant-feeding insects such as aphids and scales. They also feed on other plant secretions and on the remains of other insects, including members of their own colony. They forage in our kitchens as well, seeking out sugars as well as fats, grease, and meats. Carpenter ants produce mating swarms in the spring and are often confused with termites.

IMPACT Given the opportunity, carpenter ants readily invade houses, establishing nests in wall voids, window and door casings, insulation, and structural wood. They are also commonly found in eaves where a water problem has dampened the wood. Though they nest in both dry and damp wood, carpenter ants prefer wood with a moisture content of 15 percent or higher.

The indoor nest will be one of two types: a parental colony or a satellite colony. The latter may contain only workers, without eggs or reproductives, but will be connected to the parent colony outside. Though not as destructive as termites, carpenter ants can cause serious damage that is costly to repair.

Several signs indicate whether you are the victim of an infestation, either inside or beneath the house:

- Indoor swarms
- Foraging workers of several different sizes
- Rustling and gnawing sounds coming from the wood or wall voids
- Mounds of "sawdust"—a combination of wood, fecal material, and remnants of other ants and insects on which the carpenter ants have been feeding

CONTROL Homeowners can prevent an infestation by taking some simple precautions such as those listed below.

- Correct moisture problems, like roof and plumbing leaks.
- Clip tree limbs touching the roof to eliminate a "bridge" between ant nests and the house.
- Seal cracks in the foundation, especially around utility pipes.
- Don't allow mulch and soil to gather against the wood siding of the house.

If it's already too late to prevent an infestation, the best means to remove the ants is by finding and destroying their nests. Carpenter ants follow distinct scent trails between food sources and the nest. You can "bait" them with diluted honey, watch their movements, and follow them back to their quarters.

Once you have found their home, treat wall voids and other hidden places by carefully drilling a series of tiny holes and puffing boric acid into the nest area. Carpenter ants may also forage inside a house from an outside nest. If you find such a nest, perhaps in a stump or beneath a log, drench it with an insecticide such as carbaryl or diazinon. When using any pesticide, *always* follow the instructions on the label. Sometimes it may be necessary to contact a pest control professional.

Honey Bees

Where Have They Gone?

One of the sharpest memories of my childhood is of the night I accompanied my grandfather and two uncles Willie and Junior as they raided a bee tree for its honey. Uncle Willie had found it earlier that day while felling some trees for his woodstove. We went back after dark to get the precious golden treasure hidden in the hollow of that old oak. I was only 6 years old, but I vividly remember watching my uncles use smoke to calm the bees as they worked with hatchets and a crosscut saw to gain entrance to the hive.

Honey bees have been with people for a very long time. Early humans collected and ate the honey and honeycombs of wild bees as far back as 7000 BC, and Bronze Age communities celebrated by drinking mead, an intoxicating beverage of fermented honey. Honey bees were brought into this country in 1683 by colonists from Holland.

SCIENTIFIC NAMES Order Hymenoptera; Family Apidae; *Apis mellifera* Linnaeus

IDENTIFICATION Everyone knows what honey bees look like. Until about 15 years ago they were the dominant pollinators in our landscape, and every flowering plant teemed with industrious bee workers collecting nectar and pollen for the hive. While bees from managed hives remain fairly common, it is difficult now to find any feral bees.

BIOLOGY Honey bees are the classic social insects. Each colony, or hive, consists of a queen and her female workers. The queen is the mother of all of the workers in her hive—which may number in the thousands! Accompanied by attendants who feed and groom her, she spends her days

Honey bee populations have been greatly reduced by two mite species.

moving about the hive from brood cell to brood cell, laying an egg in each cell. Meanwhile, the workers leave the hive to forage for nectar, which will be made into honey, and for pollen, which is placed in special storage cells. The nectar and pollen stored in the hive will keep the bees alive over the winter when no food is available outside. There is almost always a surplus of honey in the fall—enough to share a bit with humans.

IMPACT We rely on honey bees to pollinate many of our crops, and their decline has serious consequences for our agriculture. For more than a decade, our honey bee populations have been decimated by two species

Honey bees are efficient pollinators.

of tiny mites whose habits could earn them the nickname "bee vampires." The varroa mite attacks mature bees, then sneaks into the brood cells and lays eggs. The young mites feed on developing bee larvae and pupae, eventually killing the entire hive. The tracheal mite enters the bee's body through a thoracic spiracle (the opening to a series of tubes called tracheae through which all insects breathe), then travels up inside these tubes and sets up housekeeping. The mites suck blood from the walls around the tracheae, lay eggs, and make themselves at home. These mites are so debilitating that honeybee swarms that escape from domestic hives rarely live more than 18 months in the wild. Bees that remain in the hives can be treated with antibiotics. Because of the effects of these mites on feral bees, some home gardeners have taken up beekeeping to ensure proper pollination for their plants.

Commercial and hobby bee keepers must treat their hives on a regular basis in order to control the mite populations in their colonies. Miticides are available for both varroa and tracheal mites, and interested individuals should contact their local extension agent.

Researchers are presently trying to breed queens that are resistant to both varroa and tracheal mites. Their offspring will likewise be resistant, and one day in the foreseeable future we may once again be treated to the sight of natural swarms of the insects that have been so important to us as pollinators and as producers of the most popular natural sweetener humankind has ever known.

Bumble Bees
Unappreciated Pollinators

All of us recognize them on sight: black and yellow, hairy, droning from flower to flower in an apparently endless search for nectar. When I was a child, my grandmother had two very large rose of sharon bushes in her backyard, and their deep blossoms were favorite nectar sources for bumble bees. That combination—deep flowers and bumble bees—also offered great sport for young boys. I and my cousins Vernon and Earl would wait until the bee had moved deep within the flower, then twist the petals closed

Bumble bees have assumed a greater role in pollinating our plants.

and break off the blossom with the bee trapped inside. We now had "live bee bombs," which we would first shake vigorously to agitate the bees and then throw at each other. (Believe it or not, I don't remember ever getting stung!)

SCIENTIFIC NAMES Order Hymenoptera; Family Bombidae; *Bombus* sp.

IDENTIFICATION About thirty species of bumble bees live in the United States. Most are robust insects ¾ to 1½ inches long. They are often confused with carpenter bees, but bumble bees are usually black and yellow with numerous hairs on the abdomen while carpenter bees have a black, shiny, hairless abdomen.

BIOLOGY Like honey bees, bumble bees are social insects, with most members working to build, feed, and protect the colony. Bumble bee colonies are much smaller, though, and do not accumulate honey. There are three types of individuals in a bumble bee colony: queens, female workers, and males. In late fall, mated queens enter underground retreats where they will spend the winter. They are able to withstand cold temperatures because they produce a natural antifreeze called glycerol that is stored in the tissues. The queens emerge in the spring to forage for nectar and seek appropriate nest sites. An abandoned rodent nest or a burrow beneath an old tree stump is prime real estate. The nest site should be dark with a generous amount of fine plant fiber. The queen collects pollen and forms it into a lump, into which she deposits six to eight eggs. After these eggs have hatched and the larvae have matured into adults (about 21 days), these new adults assume all the duties of the colony except egg laying. The nest will grow to accommodate twenty to two hundred individuals. Though the workers produce enough honey to feed the developing larvae, it never accumulates in harvestable quantities. In late summer, the colony produces future queens and males. After mating, the males leave the nest to live independent lives while the young queens remain in the hive to assist with the work of the colony. With the onset of cold weather, the queens find a place to overwinter and the cycle begins again.

IMPACT Bumble bees are among our most important and efficient pollinators. At least two species have been domesticated for use in agriculture; one is a major pollinator in greenhouses in the Netherlands and Belgium. Bumble bees are usually harmless and nonaggressive when foraging away from their nest, but they can be nasty when protecting their colony. Unlike honey bees, which can sting only once and then die, a bumble bee worker can sting repeatedly.

CONTROL If possible, bumble bee nests should be left alone because of the bees' value as pollinators. If a nest is located in a place where direct contact with humans is inevitable, control procedures should be initiated. When elimination of a colony is necessary, purchase a pressurized insecticide labeled for bee control. You should apply the material only at night, when all the workers are inside the nest. Direct the spray into the single opening to the colony. Do not aim a light directly at the opening, because the bees are attracted to lights. Check the nest opening the next day for activity and reapply if necessary.

Carpenter Bees
Grab Your Broom Handle, Junior—They're Back

Ah, spring: flowers blooming, birds singing, lovers spooning, and carpenter bees buzzing, tunneling, and destroying the outside of our home. It's one of the rites of spring. Every year we have to deal with these unwanted guests who tunnel into untreated wood on houses, decks, porches, and patios. If you have a home with unpainted wooden features, you are all too familiar with their free home renovation service. When I was a young boy, I used to spend hours near my grandfather's old barn trying to swat the hovering males out of the air with a sawed-off broom handle. Now that I'm an adult, I've discovered that a tennis racket works much better.

SCIENTIFIC NAMES Order Hymenoptera; Family Xylocopidae; *Xylocopa virginica* (Linnaeus)

IDENTIFICATION These black tunnelers resemble bumble bees and are often confused with them. Bumble bees, however, are very hairy creatures with bright yellow markings on the abdomen. Carpenter bees are ¾ to 1 inch long and have an abdomen that is shiny black with very few hairs; the males have a cream-colored mark on the face. The nesting habits of the two species are very different as well. Carpenter bee females build separate galleries for each of their young.

BIOLOGY Carpenter bee females construct their galleries in untreated wood. Each tunnel is about 6–10 inches deep. First the female bores an inch or two across the grain of the wood, then she abruptly makes a right-angle turn and finishes the burrow by tunneling another 4 inches with the grain. The bees seem to prefer to expand on tunnels from previous years. Some

Carpenter bees are serious pests of cedar homes and decks.

galleries have been in continuous use for up to 14 years and have reached lengths of up to 7 feet! The female packs the back of each tunnel with a pollen ball on which she lays an egg; then she seals off that section of the tunnel with a partition of chewed wood pulp. Additional similar cells, usually six or seven, are constructed until the tunnel is filled. Upon hatching, the developing larvae feed on the pollen until they reach maturity in about 5–7 weeks. The newly emerged adults feed, mostly on nectar, until cold weather, then seek out protected sites in which to spend the winter—sometimes in the very wooden tunnels whence they came.

The males do not build tunnels. Instead, each male stakes out a territory and aggressively defends his little empire against all comers—other bees, dogs, cats, mail carriers, and so on. Each territory may contain several active females, or queens. Some territories are better than others, of course, and the males are constantly challenging other males in an attempt to upgrade their status. When someone or something ventures too near the boundary, the male closes in and hovers aggressively, as if to say, "Get lost, buster. This is mine!" The menacing behavior is all bluff; the males are harmless because, like all male bees and wasps, they lack a stinger. I sometimes amaze my uninformed friends by snatching one out of the air and holding it captive in my hand.

IMPACT As she tunnels through the wood, the female removes the sawdust and drops it to the ground. These shavings and the sight of bees frequenting the same general area are usually the first indications that there may be a problem. The bee damage is bad enough, but if woodpeckers come a-knocking in search of the bee larvae, the damage can be much worse. When the wood is thin, as it is with cedar siding, the resulting damage can be severe. The surface holes may also offer entrance to wood-decaying fungi or other insects that attack wood, such as carpenter ants.

CONTROL For long-term control, a sound finish should be applied to the wood. Paint is the best, but preservatives with metallic salts are also effective. Selected insecticides such as diazinon or Sevin can also be applied, giving special emphasis to the tunnels themselves. If the tunnel can be treated while the bee is inside, it should be dusted and then plugged. If not, spray or dust the tunnel and plug the hole a couple of days later with putty or a caulking compound. Though swatting the males with a broom handle may not be the most effective means of control, it does offer a small measure of retribution.

Hornets

Fierce, Feisty, and Worthy of Respect

My first serious encounter with bald-faced hornets came one afternoon when I was about ten years old. My cousins Vernon and Earl and I came upon a large hornet's nest rather low in an oak tree on the banks of Blackwater Creek. A steady stream of wasps were moving in and out of the quarter-sized hole in the lower portion of the nest. Vernon searched around for a rock and hurled it at the nest. Just before he released the stone, Earl leaned towards me and whispered, "Something tells me this isn't a good idea." The rock hit the nest broadside, and the little black-and-white avengers came pouring out like steam from a boiling pot. We each suffered several stings as we beat a hasty retreat.

Bald-faced hornets are excellent predators.

Hornets are so common and so often encountered that they are part of American folklore. Many people are familiar with the old folk saying: "When hornets build nests near the ground, a harsh winter is expected." And "stirring up a hornet's nest" is still a common expression for deliberately causing trouble. These feisty, robust gangsters of the insect world, known for their powerful sting and their aggressive nature, are the mascots of numerous high schools and colleges (and even professional teams) around the country. Hornets *are* indeed more aggressive than other wasps, but only when their nest is threatened. Otherwise, they are like yellowjackets and other paper wasps. When they are foraging away from the nest, as they often do around picnic tables and pop machines, they are usually willing to leave you alone—*if* you leave them alone.

SCIENTIFIC NAMES Order Hymenoptera; Family Vespidae; *Dolichovespula maculata* (Linnaeus)

IDENTIFICATION Bald-faced hornets have a black thorax and a pale abdomen with black markings. Workers are ⅓ to ½ inch long. They have two pairs of membranous wings and are very strong flyers.

BIOLOGY Bald-faced hornets, like their cousins the yellowjackets, have an annual cycle that begins in late March when the overwintering queens emerge from their winter refuges in leaf litter, rotten logs, and other protected places and seek out suitable nest sites. The queen begins the nest and tends the first batch of "brood." After the first generation of workers emerges, she becomes an egg-laying machine and the workers do all the labor, including foraging for wood fiber to enlarge the "paper" nest.

The gray, football-shaped nests are usually at least several feet above the ground and are often built in thick vegetation such as heavily limbed trees and bushes. Though they may be quite near houses, nests are often not discovered until late in the summer when they have reached their maximum size of up to 3 feet. Large nests may contain hundreds of wasps. There is one small opening, about an inch in diameter, through which the wasps go and come. New queens and males are produced in the fall. They will mate, and the new queens will overwinter. Workers, males, and the old queen will die with the coming of cold weather.

IMPACT Hornets are very efficient predators. I have even seen them feeding on yellowjackets. They are beneficial to gardeners and homeowners, and unless they are nesting near your home or favorite recreational area, and a family member has an allergy to wasp stings, it's best to leave them alone. Hornet stings are considered more painful than those of many other bees and wasps.

CONTROL If control is necessary, extermination is the only option and should *always* be done after dark. Aim a stream of hornet spray (available in most grocery and hardware stores) directly into the small opening. Wait two or three days before removing the nest. If you are allergic to wasp stings, have someone else help you or call a pest control firm.

Yellowjackets

Unwelcome Summer Guests

The final weeks of August offer many outdoor enthusiasts their last opportunity to get away to the countryside for some fun before school begins. Unfortunately, weekend picnickers often find themselves catering to an unwanted guest—the yellowjacket. These yellow-and-black invaders appear with the first warm days of spring, and by late summer their numbers have increased to almost overwhelming proportions.

SCIENTIFIC NAMES Order Hymenoptera; Family Vespidae; *Vespula maculifrons* (Buysson); *Vespula squamosa* (Drury)

Yellowjackets can pose a serious problem when they nest in our lawns.

IDENTIFICATION The two most common Georgia species have jagged bands of yellow and black on the abdomen. They are about ½ inch long and have stouter bodies than the slender "guinea wasps" (*Polistes exclamans* (Viereck)), with which they are occasionally confused. In late summer and early fall, yellowjackets accumulate in large numbers around drink machines and trash cans, feeding on the sugary liquids in pop bottles, cans, and paper cups. They can be a serious nuisance in picnic areas because they are attracted to hamburgers and hotdogs as well as to soft drinks. They carry chunks of meat back to their underground nest to feed the young.

Yellowjackets forage on sugar.

Wasps foraging away from their nest usually will not sting unless confined or molested. The greatest danger yellowjackets pose to humans lies in accidentally disturbing their nests. These insects are extremely protective of their nest sites, and they can become painfully aggressive when an unwary visitor ventures too near the colony. Such confrontations occur most often in late spring and early summer when nests constructed in lawns and hedges are accidentally disturbed by homeowners working in their yards.

BIOLOGY New nests are started in early spring by queens that mated the previous fall. The queens, which waited out the winter under stones or rotting logs or in other retreats, emerge and search out suitable nesting sites. Their paper nests are usually built underground in abandoned rodent holes or under uprooted stumps, but occasionally a nest is made above ground between the walls of a house or in the cavities of a cinder-block wall.

Mating takes place in late fall, and newly fertilized females seek shelter for the winter.

IMPACT When a yellowjacket stings, it injects venom underneath the skin, causing pain and swelling that may last several days. The reaction may be severe or even fatal to individuals with an acute allergy to wasp stings. Ammonia or an ice pack may be placed on the area to reduce the pain and keep down swelling, and later an analgesic-corticosteroid ointment can be applied. Individuals who have an acute allergy to wasp stings should carry an epinephrine-antihistamine kit with them whenever they are out-of-doors.

CONTROL In general, these wasps are highly beneficial because they capture many harmful and destructive insects as food for their young. When large numbers come in contact with people, however, some sort of control is usually the result. Once a yellowjacket nest has been located, it can be easily destroyed by treating the nest opening, a hole in the ground about the size of a quarter, with an appropriate insecticide. Most hardware and grocery stores sell sprays labeled for wasps and hornets that will dispense a strong stream of pesticide straight into the nest opening. For nests in the walls of buildings or near certain domestic plants, use an appropriate insecticide. Treatments should be carried out after dark, when all the workers are at home. People who attempt treatments during daylight hours will receive a very hostile reception from workers returning to the nest.

Mud Daubers

Industrious Masons

Surely some of you are old enough to remember—and to have used—"outdoor plumbing." My grandfather's outhouse sat on the slope of a rather steep hill about 50 yards from the main house. Though it did not have a half moon cut into the door, it was air-conditioned enough to offer entrance and exit to various insects in the summer months, including mud daubers. I remember sitting on that wooden throne watching in amazement as these slender, industrious workers came in with mouthfuls of masonry (mud) and applied it to the walls of the outhouse. I can still hear the soft drone they made as they smoothed out the walls of their nests.

Mud daubers can be pests when they nest on manmade structures.

The organ pipe mud dauber gets its name from its "pipe organ" nests.

The Indians of the American Southwest believe that humans learned to make pottery and masonry from watching potter wasps and mud daubers. The wasps are part of southern folklore as well. I know of one folk medicine recipe that uses a tea prepared from mud dauber nests. I have no idea what this potion is meant to cure. Perhaps it's like taking a dose of castor oil—punishment for misbehaving! In the rural South, it has long been considered a very cruel act to kill a mud dauber unnecessarily.

SCIENTIFIC NAMES Order Hymenoptera; Family Sphecidae; Organ pipe mud dauber: *Trypoxylon* sp.; Black-and-yellow mud dauber: *Sceliphron caementarium* (Drury); Blue mud dauber: *Chalybion californicum* (Saussure)

IDENTIFICATION Mud daubers are slender-waisted solitary wasps that range in length from ½ to 1¼ inches. They prey on spiders. Three common species occur in Georgia. The organ pipe mud dauber, about ½ to ¾ inch long, is very shiny black and slender. This species constructs fingerlike nests of varying lengths that are attached side by side, resembling a pipe organ. The nests are often placed on roof overhangs, decks, porches, sheds, and other sheltered places. The black-and-yellow mud dauber is about 1 to 1¼ inches long and is black or dark brown with yellow markings (some yellow on the legs) and a threadlike waist. The round mud nests are often single cells or several cells placed side by side on the undersides of rocks and boards and on the walls of sheds, porches, and decks. The blue mud dauber is about ½ to ¾ inch long, thread-waisted, black to metallic blue, and has blue wings. This species makes no nest of its own, but instead pirates nests of the other two species.

BIOLOGY The female mud dauber collects moist mud and uses her mandibles to shape it into balls. She takes these chunks back to the nest site and forms tubular mud cells. Then she goes spider hunting. She first stings and paralyzes the spider, then drags it back to the nest and stuffs it into one of the mud enclosures. She lays an egg inside the cell and seals it. The developing wasp larva feeds on the paralyzed spider inside. Males may "guard" the nest while the female forages for food. Because males have no stinger, it is a token duty at best. The blue mud dauber takes over nests made by its black-and-yellow cousin. The female cleans out the spiders and the wasp eggs left by the original builder, and then often provisions her newly acquired nest with black widow spiders!

IMPACT Mud daubers are sometimes considered nuisance pests. They are not aggressive and do not protect their nests with a vengeance like other wasps. They cause a problem only when they make their mud nests in areas important to humans—on decks, porches, attics, ceilings, under eaves, and so on.

CONTROL If a nest must be removed, that is easily accomplished with a putty knife. Chemicals should be used only as a last resort because these insects are considered beneficial and rarely sting unless handled directly. The blue mud dauber is one of the most important predators of the black widow spider.

Paper Wasps

Not on the Front Porch, Please!

Each of us has a wasp story to tell, but few of them—if any—recount pleasant memories. I remember fishing one day with my old friend Danny Kinard on a farm pond in Spalding County. We were in a boat, casting to the shoreline, and my hook became entangled in a bush on the bank. We rowed in to the shore to get it, went under the overhanging limbs of the bush, and ran smack into a nest of large red wasps. I cut my line as fast as I could and we rowed back out into the lake—with one less lure and several stings apiece.

Most of the common paper wasps that we encounter on and around our homes are in the genus *Polistes*.

SCIENTIFIC NAMES Order Hymenoptera; Family Vespidae; *Polistes* sp.

IDENTIFICATION Paper wasps are sometimes confused with yellowjackets, their ground-dwelling cousins. *Polistes* wasps are generally long-legged, reddish or yellowish brown to black insects with a slender, tapered abdomen. Yellowjackets are stouter bodied, and the abdomen is broad at both ends. *Polistes* nests are usually above the ground hanging from eaves, fences, branches of trees and shrubs, and so on. Yellowjackets almost always nest underground.

BIOLOGY Queens (fertilized adult females) emerge in the spring and construct gray paper nests under eaves, on ceilings, in mailboxes, and in any other place that offers a reasonable shelter. The nest material is a mixture of chewed-up wood and saliva. Adult wasps are often seen "foraging" on old fence posts, decks, and so on, for wood they will use in nest construction.

A *Polistes* worker collects nectar.

Old nests are never reused. The nest generally has one layer of cells and is open faced and shaped like an inverted umbrella. The female begins by constructing a few honeycomb-like cells, and into each she lays an elongate, whitish egg. The eggs hatch in about 3 days, and the queen tends the developing larvae, feeding them the remains of chewed-up caterpillars and other insect prey until they seal their cells for pupation. When this brood emerges as adults, they take over the duties of nest construction, protection, and brood care while the queen produces more offspring. During the course of the summer the nest may reach a width of 8 inches and may contain up to several dozen wasps. Wasps are very protective of their nests, and this is where most stings occur. In late summer and early fall, the colony produces males and new queens. These queens mate with the males and leave the nest to find protected sites in which to pass the winter. The workers die.

IMPACT Wasps are *very* protective of their nests and are far more aggressive there than anyplace else. Individual wasps can, and will, sting several times. The stings cause local redness, pain, and swelling, although individual reactions to them vary. Emergency treatment is usually required only if a systemic (anaphylaxis) reaction occurs, in which the symptoms rapidly spread to other sites and include choking or difficulty breathing. Other symptoms include lightheadedness, nausea, stomach cramps, and diarrhea. By conservative estimates, one to two million Americans are severely allergic to stinging insect venom, and about a hundred deaths are reported each year. That number may actually be much higher because the symptoms can easily be confused with those of sunstrokes, heart attacks, or other causes.

Overwintering queens often turn up inside houses because their overwintering site led them through some crevice to the inside of the dwelling.

TREATMENT FOR STINGS

Wasp venom is acidic and can be partially neutralized by applying a base such as baking soda or ammonia. Other treatments include oral antihistamines, epinephrine inhalers (Bronkaid mist, Primatene, etc.), topical steroids (Cortaid, Lanacort, etc.), local anesthetics, and oral steroids — by prescription only.

Emergency Kits Anyone who is highly sensitive to wasp venom should carry an emergency kit containing the following: a sterile syringe containing epinephrine (adrenalin), several chewable antihistamine tablets, sterile alcohol swabs for cleaning the injection site, and a tourniquet. Inject the syringe as soon as the first sting symptoms appear.

Wasps also enter houses through an open door, a fireplace, or a heat or AC vent. Once inside, they usually crawl or fly to windows because they are attracted to light.

CONTROL Paper wasps are very beneficial insects and should not be killed unless they pose a threat to humans. They, like their yellowjacket cousins, are voracious predators and are an important part of the natural biological control that keeps many other pest species populations in check. If control is necessary, the wasps can easily be destroyed using an aerosol insecticide labeled for hornets and wasps that shoots a high-volume spray 15–20 feet, providing quick knockdown for bees and wasps.

Ladybugs
Beneficial in the Garden, Pests in the House

Many of us have childhood memories of telling little red-and-black beetles, "Ladybug, ladybug, fly away home." But as adults, in the spring and fall we now add, "but not *our* home." Though most ladybugs are considered beneficial to the landscape because they eat insect pests, several common species become nuisance pests themselves in the spring and fall when they accumulate in, on, and around buildings. Readers of my column frequently write to me regarding swarms of ladybugs on their houses.

SCIENTIFIC NAMES Order Coleoptera; Family Coccinellidae

Ladybugs are voracious predators of aphids and mites.

IDENTIFICATION Ladybugs are small, rounded beetles that come in a variety of colors, including white, pink, orange, red, and black; there are usually spots marking the back (actually the elytra — the hard covering of the wings). The introduced Asian lady beetle is about ¼ inch long, yellow-orange to dark orange-red, and often has several black spots on the back.

BIOLOGY Eggs are laid in clusters on the underside of leaves. The average time between egg and adult is about a month, and there are several generations a year. Females often lay their eggs near aphid colonies, and the larvae, which resemble tiny alligators, consume the aphids ravenously. Adults eat aphids as well, along with scale insects, mites, mealybugs, and other small, soft-bodied insects that feed on our flowers and vegetables. Adults overwinter in "swarms" beneath leaf litter and other debris. They also seek out cracks and crevices in various upright objects. It is *this* behavior that brings ladybugs into conflict with homeowners.

IMPACT The Asian lady beetle is particularly bothersome to humans because adults like to overwinter inside buildings. In the fall, these beetles are attracted to brightness, and therefore tend to congregate on the southwest (sunnier) side of buildings. Common aggregation sites include crevices around window and door frames, garages and outbuildings, beneath exterior siding and roof shingles, and within wall voids, attics, and so on. The beetles hibernate when temperatures are cold and become active when temperatures warm up in late winter and spring, often entering the inside of houses at this time through small openings.

When they are disturbed, Asian lady beetles emit a foul-smelling orange fluid that can stain walls and fabrics, so be careful when removing them from inside the house.

CONTROL Because ladybugs are useful in controlling other pests and cause little or no damage to humans or their possessions, killing them should be a last resort. Keep them from getting inside by sealing cracks and crevices around windows, doors, siding, and other entry sites. If adults come inside, remove them with a vacuum cleaner or a broom and dustpan. If you wish to release the beetles back to the outside, a handkerchief placed between the vacuum hose and the dust collection bag will act as a trap. If using a broom, remember that the beetles release a nasty defensive fluid when disturbed.

If an indoor pesticide is necessary, use it only in specific areas for immediate relief of large infestations. Aerosol foggers may be useful in attics and outbuildings but will do little to control beetles that remain in crevices. Outside applications may help prevent pest entry.

H and T Alternative Controls has developed two *very* effective traps for removing active lady beetles from buildings. Information on the traps and how to purchase them can be found at the University of Georgia's Bugwood Web site: http://www.gaipm.org/factsheets/ldybttltrap.cfm.

Aphids

If Leaves Have Honeydew, It Must Be Summer

Did you know that there are cows in your garden, and that marauding lions prey on the herd? Aphids, sometimes called "ant cows," feed on plant sap and excrete a sticky, sugary substance called honeydew. The honeydew drips from their bodies and may accumulate on leaves and stems, where it supports the growth of a black, sooty mold (actually a fungus). Some ants eat the honeydew and also "herd" the aphids and protect them from predaceous insects.

SCIENTIFIC NAMES Order Homoptera; Family Aphididae

Aphids can accumulate in large numbers on our ornamental plants.

IDENTIFICATION Aphids are ¹⁄₁₆ to ¼ inch long, with pear-shaped bodies, long antennae, sucking mouthparts, long skinny legs, and a pair of cornicles (horn-shaped tubes) on the rear of the abdomen. They come in various colors, including red, blue, black, gray, green, and yellow. Some are covered with wooly-looking wax. Aphids are the sloths of the insect world, moving with the speed of spilled molasses across the leaves and stems of their host plants. Several species are common garden pests, but they are also among the easiest to control.

Winged form of an aphid

BIOLOGY Aphids have a complicated life cycle, and its details vary greatly from one species to the next. Generally, in the fall, females lay fertilized eggs, which they glue to stems or leaves. The eggs overwinter and hatch in the spring as wingless females called "stem mothers" that reproduce parthenogenetically (without fertilization from males). The eggs hatch within their bodies and the stem mothers deposit "live young" on the plant surface. After several similar generations, some of the young aphids develop wings and migrate to other plants where they continue the asexual reproduction of wingless females. As the days grow shorter and temperatures cool, the aphids may congregate on the original plant species and produce a generation with both males and females. After mating, the females produce overwintering eggs that start the process over again the next spring.

IMPACT Aphids feeding on new growth can cause it to become distorted, twisted, curled, or swollen; severe attacks can reduce plant vigor. Sometimes aphids even kill small shoots and leaves. The honeydew can become a major problem as well. Chairs, tables, cars, and other objects beneath aphid-infested trees become covered with the sticky substance, and other insects attracted to this sugary treat can become a nuisance in their own right. When aphids move from one plant to another, they can transmit diseases through contaminated mouthparts.

CONTROL There are several options for getting rid of aphids.

- **Predators and parasites** Aphids are often kept in check by their natural enemies, which include ladybird beetles, lacewings (lacewing larvae are called "aphid lions"—I told you there were "lions" attacking "cows" in your garden!), and the larvae of syrphid flies. Tiny wasps frequently parasitize aphids, injecting their eggs into the aphid's body. The "aphid mummies" sometimes found on leaves are what remains after the wasp larvae have eaten the aphid from the inside out and the adult wasp parasites have emerged.
- **Periodic washing** A good spray with the garden hose will knock aphids off your plants and help keep the populations down. It will also allow natural enemies to work more effectively.
- **Oils and insecticidal soaps** Be sure to get complete coverage because these products have contact activity only.
- **Systemic insecticides** These are a good choice because they move through the vascular system of the plant and are taken in by the feeding aphids. Insecticides that are applied to the ground or injected into the plant are less likely to damage beneficial insects. Other contact insecticides are registered for aphids, but these should be used only as a last resort.

As the old adage says, though, an ounce of prevention is worth a pound of cure. A few horticultural practices will help keep aphids in check.

- Maintain a population of natural enemies by limiting insecticide use.
- Spray dormant oils (a very light oil especially designed for this purpose) in early spring on deciduous trees and shrubs that have shown aphid damage in the past. Spray when temperatures remain above freezing but before buds show green at the tips. Some plants are sensitive to dormant oils. Check the label for a list of sensitive species.
- Aphids love high nitrogen levels in plants, so instead of fertilizing with highly soluble nitrogen, use fertilizers like well-rotted manure or those that have slow-release nitrogen.

Bagworms

Homegrown Christmas Ornaments?

Have you noticed that some of your evergreen trees seem to be producing their
own Christmas ornaments? In some cases
these brown, spindle-shaped sacks "adorn"
the tree from top to bottom. Alas, the "or-
nament" is really the mobile home of a
moth pest called the bagworm. The larvae
manufacture their own little houses and
carry them around on their backs as they
feed. Each silken "house" is covered with
bits and pieces of twigs and leaves from
the host plant. A bagworm infestation may
go unnoticed at first, but by the time the
caterpillars are nearly grown, the branches
are often bare as a result of their feeding
and the 1–2-inch bags are clearly visible.

Bagworm cases look like shaggy
Christmas ornaments.

SCIENTIFIC NAMES Order Lepidoptera; Family Psychidae; *Thyridopteryx
ephemeraeformis* (Haworth)

IDENTIFICATION The adult male bagworm moth is about an inch long, sooty
black, and densely hairy. The larva-like adult females have neither wings
nor legs, and remain in their sacks.

BIOLOGY Bagworms overwinter as eggs inside the brown cases that hang
from the evergreen trees. The eggs hatch in late spring, and the young

larvae begin to crawl about on the host plant. As they move along, they spin threads of silk on which they drop down to other parts of the plant. Sometimes this thread acts as a "parachute" that carries the tiny caterpillar on the wind to other trees. This is the bagworm's primary means of dispersal. Each larva soon spins a silken case, leaving an opening at the head to permit crawling and feeding. As the larva grows, it continually adds bits and pieces of leaves and twigs from the host plant, increasing the size of its protective cover. When the larva is resting, the "bag" is suspended from a twig with silk. Pupation occurs in late summer and takes about a week. The adult males emerge from their bags, fly to the bags containing females, enter, and mate. Each female produces five hundred to a thousand eggs and then dies. The eggs remain in the female's body over the winter, then hatch the following spring and the cycle repeats.

IMPACT The principal injury done by bagworms is through defoliation by the caterpillar. Arborvitae, red cedar, juniper, and pine are especially susceptible, but other ornamental shrubs and trees such as maple, black locust, elm, sycamore, and rose are also eaten. Heavy infestations may kill the more vulnerable species.

CONTROL A very simple method of reducing the population is to remove the bags from infested plants and destroy the cases. This is best done in winter and early spring. The bags should be destroyed or held in containers that will allow parasites to escape into the environment. Bagworms are susceptible to low winter temperatures, and are also the targets of birds and several insect parasites. When bagworms become too numerous, a pesticide may be applied. Young larvae can be controlled effectively with Dipel, a bacterial insecticide using *Bacillus thuringiensis*. This disease affects *only* the moth larva and is very safe. Because small larvae are easiest to kill, the best time to apply insecticides is in the spring when larvae are first observed. When using any pesticide, *always* follow the instructions on the label.

Tent Caterpillars

"Cotton Candy" in Your Cherry Trees?

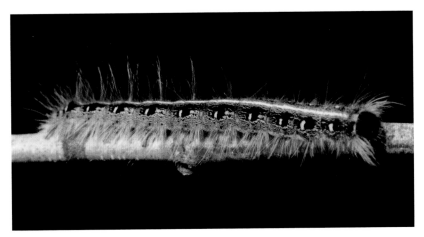

A mature tent caterpillar larva stretches out on wild cherry.

A few years ago, I received a call from a homeowner who asked, "So what's up with the cotton candy in my cherry trees?" The thick silvery masses to which the caller referred do indeed resemble wads of cotton candy, but they are far from a tasty treat. They are the silken calling card of the eastern tent caterpillar. Though the "nests" are most commonly seen in the forks of wild cherry trees, this pest can also be found in other ornamental, shade, and fruit trees, especially apples. While tent caterpillars are not a serious pest in the natural forest, an infestation can reduce the aesthetic value of shade trees and other hardwoods in the landscape.

SCIENTIFIC NAMES Order Lepidoptera; Family Lasiocampidae; *Malacosoma americanum* (Fabricius)

IDENTIFICATION Older larvae are generally black, with long brown hairs and a white stripe down the middle of the back. Along the midline is a row of blue spots with brown and yellow lines. The final instar may reach a length of 2 ½ inches. The unimpressive adult moths are not often noticed by the casual observer. They are reddish brown with two oblique stripes down each forewing.

BIOLOGY The egg masses, laid in May and early June of the previous year, are chocolate-colored collars, about an inch long, encircling the smaller limbs of the host tree, usually a wild cherry. The eggs hatch in mid-March, the same time the cherry buds unfurl, so the appearance of new leaves is like the ringing of a dinner bell. Several hundred tiny feeding machines emerge from each egg case and for 4–6 weeks hungrily strip the trees of their leaves.

The larvae are gregarious and gather in "tents" in tree forks when they are not eating. Each tent, or colony, usually includes caterpillars from several different egg masses. From this mass of silk the developing larvae move outward to feed on the tender new leaves, leaving only the midveins when they are finished. Each larva lays down a fine thread of silk wherever it crawls, and within a few days, well-defined pathways can be seen leading from the nest to various feeding sites in the tree. Most of the larvae return to the tent at night and during rainy weather, and the nest gradually becomes larger and larger, and fouler and fouler, as silk and feces accumulate. When the larvae are ready to pupate, they spin white cocoons on tree trunks or nearby objects. About 3 weeks later, the adult moths emerge, mate, and lay their eggs, which stay on the trees until the following spring, when the process begins again.

IMPACT The large silken nests in the forks of trees are unsightly. In addition, about 4–6 weeks after hatching, the full-grown larvae crawl away from the nest to look for pupation sites and accumulate on the sides of homes, in driveways, on sidewalks, and on various woody ornamentals. Homeowners worry about possible damage to other plants at this time, but the larvae have finished eating and will do no more damage.

The caterpillars are primarily a nuisance and are usually not a danger to the overall health of the tree because they finish their feeding at a time of vigorous leafing activity. Though the trees are often stripped of their leaves, they usually produce a new flush of leaves within 2 or 3 weeks.

CONTROL Usually, no control is necessary. The nests, along with their accompanying larvae, can be removed for aesthetic reasons and destroyed, and the egg masses can be clipped from the limbs in late June to prevent nests the following spring.

Fall Webworms
Another Unsightly Nuisance

"Yuck! What are those little worms that are wrapping up the leaves on my pecan tree with all that silky stuff?" Every year in late summer and early fall, unsightly whitish webs appear in trees along the roadways, and sometimes in home landscapes as well. These are the tents of the fall webworm, and they stand out against the treescape like the proverbial sore thumb. Fall webworms are not picky eaters; over their range they attack more than six hundred kinds of trees. In the South, the most common victims include pecan, mulberry, walnut, persimmon, sweetgum, and hickory.

SCIENTIFIC NAMES Order Lepidoptera; Family Arctiidae; *Hyphantria cunea* (Drury)

IDENTIFICATION The adults are small white moths, sometimes with small black spots on their wings, and are about 1 to 1½ inches long. They appear from May to August. The adults may go unnoticed, but the larvae usually do not. The caterpillars live communally in a tent of silken webbing, usually at the end of a branch. The larvae extend the silk over the leaves, keeping their food supply within the tent and themselves hidden from potential predators. Fully grown caterpillars are a little over an inch long and are covered with silky hairs. The body color varies from yellow to green to brown or black. There are two varieties of fall webworm: the larvae of one have a black head, and those of the other have a red head.

BIOLOGY Eggs are laid on the undersurface of leaves, and hatch in about a week. The small larvae immediately begin to web over single leaves and start their feeding. As they grow, they pull more leaves into the tent. At

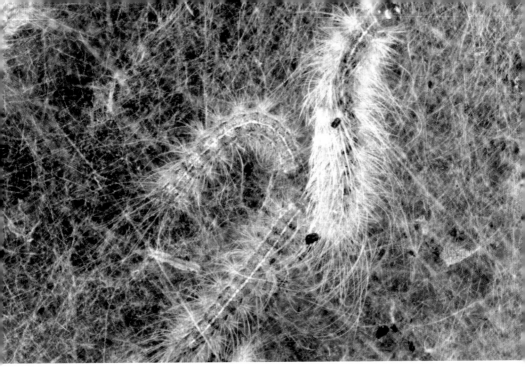

Fall webworms make unsightly webbing in our trees.

about 6 weeks of age, the larvae drop to the ground and pupate. In the South there are several generations a year.

IMPACT The unsightly webbing is usually more of a nuisance than a serious problem, but occasional severe outbreaks may defoliate shade trees. Though the webbing is primarily restricted to the tips of branches, small trees can be completely encased during outbreaks.

CONTROL Webs should be removed manually with a long stick, and the larvae destroyed. On the rare occasions when the population gets out of control, insecticides such as acephate, carbaryl, or *Bacillus thuringiensis* (a biological control agent) can be used. When using pesticides, always follow the instructions on the label.

Yellow-necked Caterpillars
What Happened to My Shade?

The sun is out, not a cloud in the sky; it's a summer day to die for. But as you stand beneath the stately oak in your backyard, it sounds as if a fine rain is steadily pelting down through the leaves. It's an eerie sensation, because what you hear does not match what you see. Instead of raindrops on the ground you see a spate of tiny black pellets, which on closer examination resemble miniature striated barrels. This is the frass (insect poop!) from the caterpillars feeding voraciously on the leaves overhead. Several species of oak pests attack our ornamental shade trees in late summer and fall. One of the most common is the yellow-necked caterpillar.

A cluster of yellow-necked caterpillars feeds.

SCIENTIFIC NAMES Order Lepidoptera; Family Notodontidae; *Datana ministra* (Drury)

IDENTIFICATION The yellow-necked caterpillar is the immature form of a moth that appears in summer. The larvae are black with yellowish stripes and are lightly covered with fine white hairs. The caterpillar gets its name from the bright orange-yellow segment directly behind its black head. Young caterpillars skeletonize the leaves, while older larvae will consume the entire leaf except for the stalk. Fully grown larvae reach a length of 2 inches. They are often found feeding in clusters, and when disturbed lift the head and tail in a distinctive U that is thought to be a defensive posture to ward off certain predatory and parasitic wasps.

BIOLOGY The moths are common in June and July and lay their eggs on the underside of the leaves of their host plants, which include oak, birch, maple, elm, and honey locust. The larvae feed in groups and are ready to pupate in August and September. Fully grown larvae drop to the ground and pupate in the soil; they emerge as adults the following summer.

IMPACT In an average year, yellow-necked caterpillars occur in relatively low numbers. You may notice some frass (are you surprised that there is actually a word for it?) on driveways, patios, sidewalks, and so on, but the caterpillars do not reach levels that produce noticeable defoliation. In some years the populations reach very high numbers, and trees will have an obvious leaf loss, even to the point of almost complete defoliation. Shade and ornamental trees are far more susceptible to this kind of damage than forest trees. Because the damage occurs late in the growing season, the trees suffer little long-term damage.

CONTROL Under normal conditions, a raft of natural predators, including beetles, birds, lizards, spiders, and parasites — mostly wasps — keep these caterpillars in check. In years when natural controls do not keep the populations under control, people have a tendency to take matters into their own hands and treat their trees with insecticides. Such treatments are difficult to do properly because special equipment is needed to spray large trees, and they are not necessarily a good idea because it is difficult to control insecticide drift when spraying tall trees. Though difficult, the best thing to do is "grit your teeth" and let nature take its course. Natural controls will eventually bring populations down, and the trees will generate new growth in the spring and will be just fine.

Hickory Horned Devils

Dragons in the Trees

It looks like a small dragon with curving, menacing horns. Its hotdog size (up to 6 inches long and ¾ inch in diameter) only adds to the threat it seems to represent—like a miniature Mothra from a 1962 B-grade horror film. When it drops unexpectedly from an overhead branch, it can send small children running and screaming to their mothers (and vice versa). And it's absolutely harmless.

SCIENTIFIC NAMES Order Lepidoptera; Family Saturniidae; *Citheronia regalis* (Fabricius)

Though hickory horned devil larvae look menacing, they are harmless.

IDENTIFICATION The hickory horned devil is the larva of the royal walnut moth (also called the regal moth), and it may drop from trees anytime between midsummer and late October. Its body color ranges from blue-green to tan. The long horns on the thorax just behind its head are black tipped with orange, and the other, shorter spikes along its back are usually black. When disturbed, this hardwood denizen rears up and tosses its head from side to side in a ferocious display intended to frighten off potential predators. The spectacular adult moth has a wingspan of 5–6 inches and a body covered with orange and yellow hairs. The wings are gray and orange with orange veins and yellow spots.

BIOLOGY In summer, regal moths emerge from pupal cases buried in the soil. After mating, females lay small clusters of eggs on the leaves of their host. Adults do not feed (they have no mouthparts) and live only a few days. Although hickory and walnut are the preferred hosts, the larvae also feed on sycamore, sweetgum, sumac, persimmon, lilac, ash, and other hardwoods. The larvae are generally invisible to humans because they feed high up in the lush green canopy overhead. In early fall, after about 40 days of feeding, they can sometimes be found crawling around on the ground. Late-developing caterpillars can survive early frosts and will continue feeding if temperatures warm up. Eventually they will burrow into the soil to pupate and overwinter. The pupal stage can last anywhere from 11 to 23 months before the adult moth emerges. Populations appear to be declining, but there are still plenty of them around, and homeowners are always quick to report them.

IMPACT Though the late-stage larvae can consume large quantities of leaves, they are rarely present in sufficient numbers to damage trees. And though their appearance is very menacing, they are totally harmless and can be handled with complete safety.

Luna Moths

Charming Guests in Your Garden

In late winter and early spring, insects begin to emerge from their winter rest to continue the cycle of life. Serious gardeners often notice only the pests that will proliferate and threaten the plants they have worked so hard to establish. But other insects come along with this warmer weather as well—harmless creatures that are arguably as beautiful as the flowers and as dainty and delicate as the gentle breeze that whispers through the garden foliage. One of these is *Actias luna*, commonly known as the luna moth.

An adult male luna moth at rest is a rare sight.

SCIENTIFIC NAMES Order Lepidoptera; Family Saturniidae; *Actias luna* (Linnaeus)

IDENTIFICATION This exquisite creature, which may reach a length of 5 ½ inches, is one of the larger silk moths in North America. Adults are light green with long, curving tails on their hind wings. All four wings have distinctive eye spots, hence the name "luna," for the "moons" on each of the wings. The body is white, and the legs are lavender-pink. Males and females are similar in appearance, although the antennae of males are larger and more feathery. These antennae carry many tiny sensors that detect pheromones—or sex attractants—released by females.

BIOLOGY Luna moths are found in all the eastern states from Maine to Florida. They appear as early as late March or April in the southern states. Adults are night fliers and float erratically on their delicate wings like tiny lime-colored angels. When they appear in well-lit public places such as baseball stadiums, they often attract a crowd because of their size and their beauty. They are more commonly seen around large sodium vapor lights positioned near forested areas. One of my favorite places on earth is the Great Smoky Mountains, and I have seen lunas floating in my headlights as I drove along the Blue Ridge Parkway after dark in the summer months. The eggs hatch into lime green caterpillars with orange spots on their sides. The larvae feed on sweetgum, hickory, sumac, persimmon, white birch, alder, and walnut. The adults do not feed and live only a few days.

IMPACT The only "damage" caused by this beautiful insect may be the quickened pulse that accompanies an encounter. The luna, though not rare, is not commonly seen because it is a night flyer.

Boxelder Bugs

Big Nuisance Inside, Little Threat Outside

Boxelder bugs can be a nuisance on the sides of our homes in the fall.

Every fall I get notes from homeowners about the little red-and-black bugs that collect on the sides of their houses. During that time of year, hundreds (sometimes thousands) of adult boxelder bugs congregate on buildings, and some get inside through cracks and crevices.

SCIENTIFIC NAMES Order Hemiptera; Family Rhopalidae; *Boisea trivittatus* (Say)

IDENTIFICATION Adult boxelder bugs are about a half-inch long, slate gray in color, and have three red stripes behind the head and red lines on the wings. The rear margin of the wings is reddish, and the abdomen beneath the wings is also red, as are the eyes. Nymphs (the wingless preadult stages) are very bright red with a darker head.

BIOLOGY In late summer and fall, adult and large nymph boxelder bugs gather in large numbers, usually on the bark of boxelder trees, before either flying or crawling to a suitable sanctuary for the winter. They seek and find almost any crack or crevice — in walls, door and window casings, rock piles, tree holes, and in the foundations of houses. On warm winter days they emerge and rest on the south or west side of the house, usually on white or very light surfaces. If they have access to the inside, they may also appear there in large numbers, making nuisances of themselves and alarming the homeowner.

Adults emerge from their winter sanctuaries in March and early April and feed for about 2 weeks prior to mating. Females lay their eggs in cracks and crevices near host plants. The light yellow eggs quickly turn rusty red and hatch in about 2 weeks. Nymphs appear about the time that new leaves emerge on host plants. In addition to boxelder, this insect feeds on apple, ash, buckeye, maple, plum, cherry, peach, and grape, as well as other ornamentals. Around the middle of July, new adults lay eggs for a second generation that will mature by early autumn.

IMPACT Boxelder bugs feed primarily on boxelder and maple seeds, and also suck sap from the leaves and twigs, but they do little damage to their primary hosts. Because of their fall invasion of homes, they are more commonly considered a household pest. There are conflicting reports regarding whether they bite when handled carelessly, but if they do bite, it is not a common occurrence. Their fecal material may stain wallpaper, upholstery, curtains, and other furnishings, and they may emit a repugnant odor when crushed.

CONTROL It is *very* difficult to control boxelder bugs *after* they have gotten into the house. Individual bugs can be removed by hand or with a vacuum cleaner. Household sprays containing pyrethroids will kill them on contact. It is far better to prevent the bugs from getting in by using weather stripping to seal all cracks and crevices through which they may gain admittance. Windows, including those in the attic, should have screens or storm windows. Vents in soffits and crawl spaces should also be screened. When they aggregate in the fall, boxelder bugs are vulnerable to insecticides, which can eliminate a great many at one time. Eliminating harborages like rock piles, lumber, and leaves that have accumulated near the house will also help to control them.

Because female boxelder trees are the single most important food source for these insects, removing female trees will greatly reduce numbers of boxelder bugs. Usually, populations are not large enough to warrant the use of pesticides, but if they are needed for use on gregarious clusters, contact your local extension agent for recommendations.

Euonymus Scales
Measles Mean a Big Problem

When I was a young faculty member at the Georgia Experiment Station in Griffin, a caller said that his euonymus plants had a bad case of the measles. He had euonymus scales. My department head, Dr. Ham Tippins, one of the most versatile and best-informed entomologists I have ever known, told him that the best control for euonymus scales was to cut down the euonymus and replace it with something else. At the time that was not a bad solution. There were few if any resistant euonymus varieties, and other control procedures were not very effective because scale populations often reached numbers sufficient to kill the host plant.

SCIENTIFIC NAMES Order Homoptera; Family Diaspididae; *Unaspis euonymi* (Comstock)

IDENTIFICATION Euonymus scales are small, juice-sucking insects with paperlike armor that protects them from many predators and insecticides. The sacklike adult females are rarely seen because they remain beneath these coverings, which are dark brown, about 1/16 inch long, and resemble tiny oyster shells. The male's armor is white, slightly smaller, a bit more elongate, and has three longitudinal ridges. Adult males are small, winged insects that leave their tiny suits of armor in search of females for mating.

BIOLOGY Adult female euonymus scales settle mainly on stems but are also found on the leaves of their host. Males are usually restricted to the underside of leaves and to lower branches. Fertilized adult females overwinter and lay eggs in late March and early April beneath their protective covers. The newly hatched "crawlers" form the only mobile stage (except the adult

Note the white pupal cases of the euonymus scale males on this leaf.

male, which does not feed). These tiny insects emerge from beneath their mother's armor and move around on the plant. They find a spot to settle down, insert their long mouthparts into the plant tissue, begin to feed, and develop papery coverings of their own. Each time the juvenile insect molts, the previous cast skin is incorporated into the new "shell" of the next instar. There are often three generations a year in Georgia. First instars emerge in late March, June, and August.

IMPACT A severe scale infestation can totally encrust the stem of the host and can eventually kill the plant. Even if the scales do not kill the host, their appearance is unsightly, and in large numbers they can cause the leaves to yellow and drop.

CONTROL Homeowners who like euonymus as an ornamental should consider planting varieties resistant to this scale; *Euonymus alatus 'Compactus'* and *E. fortunei 'Acutus'* are among the most successful. This insect is *very* difficult to control. When the infestation is relatively light, the more heavily infested branches can be pruned out, or the scales themselves can be scraped off by hand and destroyed. Unless a particular plant is very valuable and heavily infested, insecticides should not be used because they will have a negative effect on naturally occurring parasites and predators that feed on this pest. A light oil can be used to control crawlers. When using oils, *always* follow the directions on the label; misuse may damage plants. If insecticides must be used for crawler control, check with your county extension agent for suggestions.

Hornworms

Attack of the Tomato Killers

Your tomatoes are growing nicely. The leaves are green and full, and small fruits are popping out all over the plants. One morning you go outside to water your plants, and one of them looks like Sherman has returned for another march to the sea. Something has almost completely stripped the leaves, leaving nothing but bare stems and a stalk. Even some of the tiny tomatoes have been partially eaten. A close examination of the plant reveals a fat green caterpillar, the color of the tomato plant, clinging to one of the stems. You have been victimized by a tomato hornworm.

SCIENTIFIC NAMES Order Lepidoptera; Family Sphingidae; *Manduca quinquemaculata* (Haworth)

A tomato hornworm feeds on tomato leaves.

IDENTIFICATION Tomato hornworms are the larvae of a species of hawk moth. These moths resemble hummingbirds and are easily confused with them. They fly at dusk and at night and frequently hover around flowers, feeding on nectar with their elongate mouthparts. The fat green larvae reach a length of 3–4 inches and have seven white diagonal slashes down both sides of the body. The name "hornworm" comes from the presence of a black or red "horn" that extends upward from the rear end.

BIOLOGY Adult moths appear in May and June and mate soon afterward, and females lay their yellow-green eggs on the underside of leaves. The eggs hatch in 6–8 days and the larvae feed for several weeks. When fully grown, the larvae burrow into the soil and pupate. The large brown pupa stays in the soil all winter. In late spring, the adults emerge and the life cycle begins anew.

IMPACT The voracious caterpillars can consume large quantities of leaves in a short time. Their cryptic color provides excellent camouflage, and despite their large size they are difficult to spot. They feed on the leaves and young stems (and sometimes the fruit) of a variety of related plants, including tomatoes, eggplants, peppers, potatoes, and tobacco.

CONTROL

Natural Control Hand picking offers good control in a small home garden *if* you can locate the intruders. Examine the plants carefully in July and August, especially if you notice leaf damage. Occasionally, hornworms are observed with many tiny white projections sticking out from their bodies. These are cocoons of a small parasitic wasp. The wasp larvae eat the inside of the hornworm, then emerge to the outside to pupate. (The hornworm larva does not survive the experience.) Such cocoon-laden larvae should not be killed because they provide more wasps that will seek out other hornworms in the garden.

Chemical Control When an outbreak of hornworms occurs, dusts and sprays can be applied evenly over the tomato foliage. Contact your local county extension office for the most recent recommendations. When using pesticides, *always* follow the instructions on the label.

If you wish to be both frugal *and* efficient in your control efforts, you may wish to follow this recipe from *The Eat-a-Bug Cookbook* (Web site http://www.davidgeorgegordon.com/). The author, D. G. Gordon, says he drew his inspiration from the cuisine of the fictitious "Whistle Stop Cafe" of novelist Fannie Flagg.

Fried Green Tomato Hornworms

3 tablespoons olive oil

16 tomato hornworms

4 medium green tomatoes, sliced into ¼-inch rounds

salt and pepper to taste

white cornmeal

In a large skillet or wok, heat the oil. Then lightly fry the hornworms over high heat, about 4 minutes, taking care not to rupture the cuticle of each insect. Remove with a slotted spoon and set aside.

Season tomato rounds with salt and pepper, then coat with cornmeal on both sides.

In a large skillet, fry tomatoes until lightly browned on both sides.

Top each round with 2 fried tomato hornworms.

Garnish the paired hornworms with a single basil leaf.

Bon appétit!

Vine Borers and Pickleworms

Watch for Them in Summer Squash

Whether we live in "big city busy" or rural country calm, many of us are driven to smell moist, turned earth and taste fresh vegetables from our own backyard garden. Nothing tastes quite as good as something personally grown and harvested. Among the most popular spring and summer vegetables in home gardens are yellow squash and zucchini. Their flowing greenery and opulent blooms provide aesthetic beauty as well as tasty garden fare. So it is doubly frustrating to suddenly discover that many of our squash vines have abruptly withered and their beautiful greenery is fading rapidly in the morning sun.

SCIENTIFIC NAMES Order Lepidoptera; Squash vine borer: Family Sesiidae; *Melittia cucurbitae* (Harris); Pickleworm: Family Pyralidae; *Diaphania nitidalis* (Stoll)

IDENTIFICATION The adult squash vine borer is a small, clear-winged moth that superficially resembles a wasp. The pickleworm moth, also small, has a large yellow spot in the center of its front wings and a wide brown border on its hind wings.

BIOLOGY The squash vine borer moth lays her eggs on the plant stems. The newly hatched larvae

A squash vine borer in a squash

Squash vine borers can cause much damage in your garden.

bore into the stem and grow rapidly, maturing in about a month. There are two generations a year in the South. The pickleworm moth lays eggs on the foliage, and the young larvae feed on small leaves before boring into the fruit itself. Pickleworms appear a bit later than squash vine borers because they migrate northward from South Florida.

IMPACT Squash vine borer larvae often begin their journey through the stem at the base of the plant, but can travel upward almost to the leaves. Stems are sometimes girdled, preventing water and nutrients from circulating in the plant, and injured vines often decay and look wet and shiny. The first sign of damage is usually a pile of yellow excrement, like sawdust, that falls from holes in the stem. Pickleworm larvae can be detected with the use of a 10x hand lens. If this pest is suspected, open up the newly developing leaf and flower buds. If the larvae are present, they will be inside.

CONTROL Different techniques are called for to rid plants of the two pest species.

Squash Vine Borer If you have only a few vines, watch them carefully for wilting. If it appears, check the base of the plant for signs of excrement and borer damage. Remove the borer by cutting a slit in the vine with a sharp knife. Cover the injured area with moist soil. You may wish to put a shovelful of soil at several spots along each vine to encourage the plant to develop a supplementary root system and thus overcome some of the damage. Always destroy old vines after the harvest to destroy any larvae or pupae still in the vines.

Pickleworm Watch for larvae in newly developing leaf and flower buds. Holes in fruits indicate heavier infestation. If you want to use insecticidal control for summer squash, preventive treatments are best. Apply pesticides when vines begin to run, and continue on a 7–10-day schedule for 3–5 weeks. Sevin works fairly well for both species. For other choices, contact your local county extension agent.

Lace Bugs

Far from Fragile

Lace. The word conjures thoughts of soft, delicate, and fragile things. Curtains, perhaps, or handkerchiefs, tablecloths, and lingerie. The name "lace bug" might bring that same fragility to mind: they must be tiny, delicate, and harmless creatures. But where lace bugs are concerned, thoughts of Joseph Kesselring's *Arsenic and Old Lace* would be more appropriate. Lace bugs are definitely tiny; and they do look fragile. The wings and parts of the thorax are covered

"Dainty" lace bugs can be trouble.

with a lacelike network of veins and membranes. Under a microscope, their beauty rivals that of an antique lace handkerchief. But these little demons can cause excessive damage to their host plants, and the homeowner should be aware of—and wary of—the consequences of their feeding.

SCIENTIFIC NAMES Order Hemiptera; Family Tingidae

IDENTIFICATION Lace bugs have piercing-sucking mouthparts and feed on the plant juices found in the leaves of their hosts. Most of them live on the underside of the leaves. The adults are only about ⅛ to ¼ inch long. The immature forms do not show the lacy pattern of the adults and appear flat and spiny.

BIOLOGY The eggs hatch in late March to early April, and the immature stages go through five nymphal instars before reaching adulthood. It takes approximately 1 month for the insect to complete development from egg to adult. There are usually three to five generations a year. The azalea lace bug overwinters as eggs on the underside of leaves.

IMPACT Lace bugs are pests of a number of broad-leaved evergreens such as azalea, rhododendron, pyracantha, and laurel. Other popular shrubs like cherry, adromeda, cotoneaster, and alder are also attacked. Some shade trees are vulnerable as well, including oak, birch, willow, sycamore, and hawthorne. Heavy feeding gives the leaves a stippled appearance, and the underside of the leaf is usually covered with dark fecal spots, or "tar spots," along with cast skins and various developmental stages of the insect. Very heavy feeding will turn the leaves yellow and often causes them to drop prematurely. If the heavy infestation lasts most of the season, death of the plant is also a possibility.

CONTROL Choosing an appropriate planting site is a good way to start. A susceptible plant placed in an inappropriate environment may be more subject to damage by lace bug feeding. Azaleas and rhododendrons in low or moderately acid soil, in direct sunlight, or under water stress will be more apt to suffer attack.

Chemical control, if needed, should be applied to infested plants before lace bugs build up in large numbers. After the population has gotten out of hand, chemical control may be the only alternative. Lace bug populations should be monitored regularly. Spot treatment of infested hosts is preferable to areawide spraying. Contact your local county extension office for the most recent recommendations. Read the label *carefully* for appropriate dosage rates and other precautions.

Spittlebugs

Frothy Masses in Your Grasses?

I'll never forget the first time I mowed my "new" lawn in Athens, Georgia. The lawn was "new" because I had just purchased a home and it was the first time I had the "privilege" of mowing it. I immediately noticed a large number of reddish black "things" billowing out from beneath the mower and stopped to take a look. Several dozen insects, killed by the swirling blade, had fallen into the depression on top of the mower.

Two-lined spittlebugs are rarely pests.

On closer examination of the lawn itself, I saw little frothy masses down in the blades of the centipede grass. The insects on the lawnmower were adults of the two-lined spittlebug, and the "spittle" in the grass hid the immature stages.

SCIENTIFIC NAMES Order Homoptera; Family Cercopidae; Two-lined spittlebug: *Prosapia bicinta* (Say)

IDENTIFICATION The adult spittlebug is about ¼ to ⅜ inch long, black, and has two red or orange lines across the wings. The wingless nymphs, usually hidden in their frothy sanctuary, are yellow, orange, or white with a brown head.

BIOLOGY Spittlebugs overwinter as eggs behind leaf sheaths, in plant debris, or in hollow stems. Humidity is an important factor in spittlebug development. Both eggs and immature stages need a moist environment. Nymphs hatch out in May or June. They usually settle deeper into the turf and soon produce a mass of frothy spittle that protects them both from natural enemies and from desiccation. The nymphs go through four stages over a period of about a month before becoming adults. The adults are most active early in the day and spend the warmer hours deep in the turf. They are rousted out when one mows the grass, however, and fly out from beneath the mower like tiny black pebbles.

IMPACT Though usually not a serious pest in well-managed turf, spittlebugs can become a problem during periods of high humidity. Both adults and nymphs penetrate the plant tissue with their piercing mouthparts and suck out the sap. The grass may wilt and fade from green to yellow to brown. Some of the grass may die, giving the lawn a splotchy appearance. Damaged areas often begin as yellow or brown patches about 2–5 inches in diameter.

The adults feed on a variety of ornamentals, including hollies, blackberry, and morning glory. The nymphs are most common in grasses, and are most damaging to centipede, Saint Augustine, zoysia, and some Bermudas. Damage usually begins in June and continues into early September.

CONTROL Control measures are often unnecessary if the lawn is under a good maintenance program. Dethatching and fertilization can disrupt the humid conditions necessary for spittlebugs to thrive. When treatment is required, mow the lawn and destroy all clippings before the insecticide is applied. Treatment should be done late in the day. Contact your local county extension office for the most recent pesticide recommendations.

Wheel Bugs

Modern-Day Garden Dinosaurs

Those who have seen the movie *Jurassic Park* or one of its various incarnations (i.e., most of us) know that *Tyrannosaurus rex* was the most fearsome predator of its day. Let's fast-forward to the present in your backyard. Imagine *T. rex* with a long, heavy piercing beak instead of teeth—a beak on which it impales its prey and through which it injects powerful digestive enzymes to break down the tissues of its victims. Then it sucks their bodies dry. To a slow-moving caterpillar sliding through the foliage jungle of a garden, that is exactly how the wheel bug appears.

The adult wheel bug is the *Tyrannosaurus rex* of the insect world.

The bloodsucking species in this family are active at night and usually feed on sleeping victims. One species that is very common in Mexico and Central and South America is a vector of Chagas' disease, a very nasty form of trypanosomiasis. This disease is not common in the United States because there are no efficient vectors here, but it does pose a possible future health concern.

SCIENTIFIC NAMES Order Hemiptera; Family Reduviidae; *Arilus cristatus* Linnaeus

IDENTIFICATION The wheel bug is one of a number of species in a family commonly referred to as "assassin bugs." All of them are exclusively predaceous. Some are bloodsucking parasites of mammals, including humans, while many others feed on a wide variety of garden pests. All are characterized by a long, narrow head; a short, stout, three-segmented beak; and long, slender antennae. A mature wheel bug is 1 to 1 ½ inches long, grayish black, and has an upright, semicircular "cog wheel" crest on the thorax with eight to twelve protruding teeth. It is the only insect in the United States with such a crest. Its large eyes and uncommonly stout beak give it a very ominous appearance. Nymphs are bright red with black markings and are usually found in April and May. Only the adults have the characteristic cogged crest.

BIOLOGY The wheel bug produces only one generation a year and overwinters in the egg stage. Some adults survive at least part of the winter and are occasionally seen even in December. After the eggs hatch in spring, the development time to adulthood is about 3 months. Under natural conditions both nymphs and adults are *very* aggressive predators. In a closed environment, they will feed on their own species, and females have been reported to devour males soon after copulation is complete. (Talk about a horror movie . . .) The wheel bug feeds by impaling its victim with its stout beak, then injecting potent saliva into its body. The enzymes in the saliva quickly subdue the prey and digest the inside tissues. The bug then sucks in this digested liquid.

IMPACT Menacing appearance aside, the wheel bug is a genuine friend to the backyard gardener. It is a voracious predator that feeds on many of our common garden pests. Though reluctant to attack humans, wheel bugs can inflict a very painful bite when disturbed. The pain comes from the enzymes in the saliva, and can be much worse than stings from bees, wasps, and hornets. The initial pain is followed by numbness that may last for several weeks, depending on one's sensitivity to the saliva.

CONTROL Because wheel bugs are important predators in the garden and because populations are usually rather low, leave them alone if at all possible! Avoid direct contact because they may bite if handled. If they become a nuisance, they can be killed individually.

Whiteflies

Are the Gardenias Smoking?

The steps leading to my deck are guarded by two large gardenia bushes. As I was walking down to the yard one spring day, I brushed against some new growth. Immediately, a large white plume rose up from the gardenias like heavy smoke. Whiteflies! At first glance, these tiny creatures resemble tiny moths: delicate, dainty, and totally harmless. But don't let their size fool you. Like termites, they can build up tremendous numbers, and their cumulative effect on your plants can be devastating. Though several species are found on gardenias, the most common one in the Atlanta area is the citrus whitefly. It is found from Virginia south to Florida and west through Texas to California.

SCIENTIFIC NAMES Order Homoptera; Family Aleyrodidae; Citrus whitefly: *Dialeurodes citri* (Ashmead)

IDENTIFICATION Whiteflies are not flies. Although adults resemble tiny white moths, they are actually close relatives of scale insects, aphids, and leafhoppers. Like their cousins, whiteflies suck plant juices from their hosts. Adults have a "mealy" appearance that results from powdery wax produced by glands on the abdomen. It is from this waxy covering that they get the name "whiteflies." They have four white wings that span less than ⅛ of an inch and are held almost flat against the body when not in use.

Adult whitefly

Whiteflies often accumulate on the underside of leaves.

BIOLOGY Adults are usually found on the underside of leaves, and often the first sign of an infestation is a cloud of tiny white insects that rises up like heavy smoke when you brush against a plant in the garden. Females lay tiny yellow eggs on the underside of the leaves, partially inserting them into the leaf surface. The eggs hatch in 1–3 weeks, and the pale green crawlers immediately seek a place to insert their mouthparts. The crawlers look a lot like scale insects, and like many scales, once they settle and begin to feed, they become totally immobile. Immature whiteflies excrete a sugary substance called honeydew as they feed, and this promotes the growth of a sooty mold fungus that can cover the leaf surface. In the Atlanta area, there are two generations, one emerging in April and the other in late summer.

Whitefly larvae congregate on the underside of a leaf, where they feed.

IMPACT Whitefly nymphs remove large amounts of sap from the leaves on which they feed, and heavy infestations can greatly reduce the vigor of plants. The sooty mold that grows on the honeydew produced by the immature stages can both affect photosynthesis and reduce the aesthetic value of plants.

CONTROL Because all stages are commonly found on the *underside* of the leaves, whiteflies can be difficult to control. A good control program should start with a dormant oil spray in late winter or early spring. Insecticides like Orthene or Cygon can be sprayed for effective control. Insecticidal soaps are an environmentally friendlier alternative, but these kill *only* the whiteflies they contact, so thorough coverage is essential.

White Grubs

Don't They Make Your Green Lawn Brown

The month of June holds many special memories from my childhood. Among them: the beginning of summer vacation, swimming in Blackwater Creek, fishing in the James River, and competing in the annual green June beetle kite-flying contests. We would tie a long piece of Mom's sewing thread to the back leg of a green June beetle, then toss it into the air. The beetle would fly upward as we ran gleefully beneath, our living kites pulling gently at the ends of their delicate tethers. The one whose beetle flew the highest was declared the winner. Of course, we had no idea that this bright green, foul-smelling creature was the adult form of the "grub worm" we used for fish bait, or the underground pest that ate the roots of our lawn

White grubs are beetle larvae and can cause major damage to turf.

grasses. In fact, the immature forms of a number of scarab beetles, including the green June beetle, Japanese beetle, May beetles, and chafers, are important pests of turf and occasionally require control to prevent serious injury to lawns.

SCIENTIFIC NAMES Order Coleoptera; Family Scarabeidae; Green June beetle: *Cotinus nitida* (Linnaeus); Japanese beetle: *Popillia japonica* Newman; May beetles: *Phyllophaga sp.*

BIOLOGY All of these beetles have a similar life history, with slight variations in timing. Adults emerge and mate in late spring and early summer. Egg laying commences soon after that, and the larvae hatch in June and July. Grubs generally reach maturity in late summer, and do most of their damage in early fall. As cold weather approaches, the larvae dig deeper in the soil to overwinter; they come up again in spring with the warmer temperatures.

IMPACT Root-feeding white grubs damage turf, which often wilts and dies. The sod itself can become loose, and occasionally can be rolled up like a carpet. Green June beetle larvae feed primarily on decaying vegetation rather than grass roots. Their extensive tunneling produces a spongy layer in the soil up to 2 inches deep. The tunnels disturb the contact between the soil and the plant roots, interfering with water uptake and causing the plants to die. Green June beetle larvae are the only ones that come out onto the surface at night and move across the ground on their backs. This behavior brings them more readily into contact with pesticides and makes them among the easiest of the white grubs to control.

Although all grasses are possible targets, bluegrass and bent grass are especially vulnerable. Symptoms are sometimes masked during periods of rapid turf growth and adequate water, and it's thus a good idea to examine sod periodically. The sight of birds feeding on the lawn can be an indication that grubs are present. To be sure, a survey is necessary. Water the soil thoroughly the day before the survey if conditions are dry. Use a heavy spade or knife to cut several 1-square-foot flaps of sod, cutting along three sides of each and rolling the turf back like a rug to reveal the top 2–4 inches of soil. The grubs will be C-shaped, cream-colored larvae with brown heads and a darker area at the posterior end. Lawns with an average of five to eight grubs per square foot may require treatment.

CONTROL Control is best achieved in late summer when most of the eggs have hatched but the larvae are still relatively small. If the ground is dry, water before applying an insecticide for white grubs. This will force the larvae closer to the surface. For specific soil pesticide recommendations, contact your local county agent.

Fireflies

Fairy Lanterns in the Backyard

Fireflies. Lightningbugs. Whatever you call them, the name conjures fond memories of childhood. Summer nights: running through the backyard trying to catch up with the little flying lanterns silhouetted against the night sky. When I was growing up in Campbell County, Virginia, I used to compete with my cousins Vernon and Earl to see who could catch the most lightningbugs. We'd put them in jars and gape in amazement at the beautiful luminescence the little creatures produced. Later, we might put the jars by our beds as "night lights." (It has been said that three dozen fireflies can produce as much light as a small candle.) And — yes — we would occasionally mash them on our skin, making "glow-in-the-dark" streaks across our faces to frighten our playmates — especially the girls.

Fireflies have a tiny "lightbulb" at the tip of their abdomen.

Firefly populations may seem to have dwindled, but for the most part they are still here. It's just that we don't see them as much as we used to. Years ago, there were fewer lights to compete with their glow: no shopping centers, no large mercury vapor lights on each street corner. And our cultural activities have changed as well. Today, adults and children are not as apt to be outside in the early evening darkness chatting with neighbors, sitting on front porches, or running free across lawns and fields, capturing these little insects for their jars. Most of us now spend our evenings inside, surfing the Web or watching TV.

SCIENTIFIC NAMES Order Coleoptera; Family Lampyridae; Big Dipper firefly: *Photinus pyralis* (Linnaeus)

IDENTIFICATION Lightningbugs are not "bugs" at all; they are small, soft-bodied beetles with an extended pronotum that gives them a "hooded" appearance. Adults are about ¾ inch long, with long, soft, blackish wings. They are best identified by the little "lightbulb" at the rear of the abdomen. And most important—to the fireflies, anyway—they can turn this light on and off at will. There are about 125 species in the United States, but the Big Dipper firefly is by far the most common.

BIOLOGY Lightningbugs overwinter in the soil as larvae and emerge in spring. They are predaceous, feeding on whatever they can catch, including various insects, caterpillars, earthworms, and even each other. Some lightningbug larvae also produce light and are called "glow worms." In early summer, the larvae pupate, and in about 2 weeks the adults emerge. They, too, are highly predaceous. It is this stage that has captured the imagination of generations of children—and the adults they become—as we remember fondly those special moments of our childhood. The males fly about in the early evening dusk looking for females (reminds me of my own adolescence, but that's another story . . .), who are usually perched on low vegetation, flashing their lights to attract mates. Different species flash with different frequencies, and when a male sees a flashing light that matches his search profile, he moves in. Usually, this story has a happy ending. Mating takes place, eggs are laid, and the cycle starts over. But sometimes the transmitted signal is produced by another firefly species that is mimicking the flash frequency. When the hapless male enticed by the flashes lands nearby, this "femme fatale" snags him for supper.

In some parts of the world, fireflies flash in synchrony and the results are spectacular. In Southeast Asia, members of a tropical species congregate in trees and flash on and off like Christmas lights. Recently this phenomenon has been documented in the Smoky Mountains near Elkmont, Tennessee.

IMPACT Aside from the sheer enchantment of their presence, these little creatures are very beneficial garden residents because both larvae and adults are predaceous. They have commercial value as well; large numbers are harvested annually by the biochemical industry. The firefly "lightbulbs" contain luciferin and the enzyme luciferase, compounds useful in testing food for bacterial contamination, evaluating the effectiveness of certain medications, and assisting in gene coding.

Asian Tiger Mosquitoes

Backyard Nuisance and Health Concern

By day or by night they will try to eat you alive. A single one in a still, dark room can create mental torment with its characteristic chopped-off *eeeeeeeeeaaaagnt!* just outside your ear. You know it's a mosquito, you know it has landed somewhere on your body, and you know it wants your blood. In swarms, they can force picnickers and backyard cooks inside.

The Asian tiger mosquito is a stealthy, aggressive biter that brings both physical discomfort *and* a major threat of disease. In just a few years it has

Mosquitos offer both physical discomfort and the threat of disease.

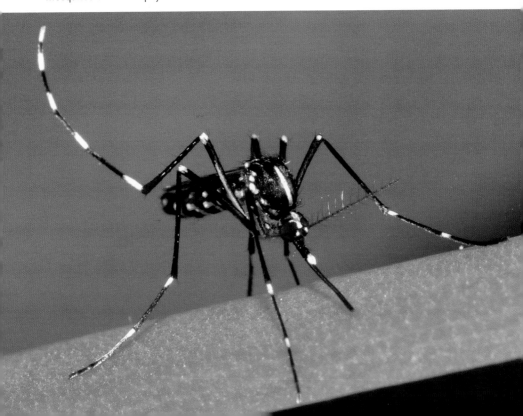

become one of Atlanta's dominant mosquito species. The tiger mosquito is a native of the Orient and is common from New Guinea westward to Madagascar, northward through India and Pakistan, and through China and northern Japan. It arrived in the United States in the late 1980s, apparently in a shipment of tires from Japan, and interstate commerce of used tires has spread this mosquito to many new locations.

SCIENTIFIC NAMES Order Diptera; Family Culicidae; *Aedes albopictus* (Skuse)

IDENTIFICATION The adult female (the only stage that feeds on blood) is slightly less than ¼ inch long and is dark black with bright white markings. The thorax has a distinct white "racing stripe" down the middle, the abdomen has broken white stripes that may appear as white dots, and the legs are striped with snow white scales.

BIOLOGY This mosquito is commonly known as a "containment breeder" because it lays eggs in small patches of water in tin cans, spare tires, and flower pots rather than in swamps or marshes as most of its mosquito brethren do. The eggs are glued to the sides of these containers and need a period of drying before they hatch. When rain or another water source raises the level of water in the container, the eggs hatch and the mosquitoes develop from larvae to adults in the container. This species probably originated in a forest setting, where it bred in tree holes or leaf axils of epiphytic plants. Because a portion of the population still follows the same habit, it is very difficult to control.

IMPACT This species is an aggressive biter, and its common name may well refer as much to its nature as to its white stripes. Tiger mosquitoes are opportunistic feeders that bite readily during the day as well as at dusk. In recent years this species has largely replaced the yellow fever mosquito in most areas of the southern United States. In addition to being a serious nuisance pest, it is also a vector of several dangerous diseases, among them dengue, eastern equine encephalitis, and La Crosse encephalitis. Dengue, or breakbone fever, was a sporadic problem in the southern United States before being eradicated in the 1940s, and the introduction of the Asian tiger mosquito has raised concerns about renewed outbreaks. But since reappearing in Texas in the mid-1980s, no additional cases of dengue have been reported. La Crosse encephalitis is another matter. This is a viral disease that attacks the central nervous system and is found primarily in children under fifteen. The Asian tiger mosquito has been linked to a high percentage of the identified cases of La Crosse encephalitis in the Southeast. Although most infections are asymptomatic or appear only as a mild flu-like illness, the few cases that come to the attention of the public are serious and require emergency room visits and intensive care. Fever, headache, vomiting, and behavioral changes are the primary symptoms, and seizures and loss of consciousness are possible.

CONTROL Because it breeds in tiny stagnant pools, the Asian tiger mosquito is very difficult to control. Even a small pool makes an excellent egg-hatching area. Remove all objects that may allow water to collect, such as tin cans, plastic buckets, bottles, and old tires. Empty watering cans and children's pools if they are not used frequently. Change the water in bird baths. Even flower pots should be monitored to keep standing water to a minimum. Tree holes may be drained and filled with mortar or sand and covered with Treekote or other material.

For control around patios and decks, spray pyrethrins or fog with resmethrin. If you are going to be outside, especially at dusk, in areas where mosquitoes are active, always wear a repellent containing DEET. When using pesticides, *always* follow the instructions on the label.

Lubber Grasshoppers
Usually Harmless Giants

Sometimes it seems that they rise up from the very crypts themselves, by the hundreds, even thousands, lumbering along like zombies from some B-grade horror movie. Even in the face of their enemies they move onward, fearless and oblivious to danger. Residents whose homes and gardens are located near or at the site of a major emergence for the eastern lubber grasshopper do sometimes feel like they are being invaded by the undead.

SCIENTIFIC NAMES Order Orthoptera; Family Acrididae; *Romalea guttata* (Houttuyn)

IDENTIFICATION Adult males and females of the lubber grasshopper, sometimes locally called cemetery grasshoppers because of their propensity to appear in very large numbers in and around cemeteries, are about 2 ½ and 3 inches long, respectively—very big for a grasshopper. Their color varies from black with yellow or red markings to dull yellow with varying degrees of black. Nymphs, which lack wings, are typically black with distinctive yellow stripes, and their front legs and the sides of the head are often red. The common name, "lubber," is an excellent choice because this summer visitor does indeed appear slow, clumsy, and awkward. The wings are very short, and even adult lubbers are incapable of flight. Therefore, this "lumbering giant" goes from plant to plant by moving slowly over the surface of the ground.

BIOLOGY Lubber grasshoppers have one generation a year, with the first eggs hatching in March and April. There are five instars prior to the adult, each lasting about 15–20 days. Females lay their eggs in the summer months

Large in size, lubber grasshoppers are often used in biology labs.

about 2 inches beneath the soil surface. Adults occur in largest numbers in July and August. Though lethargic, these easygoing creatures are well protected from their enemies. Ready for today's five-dollar word? It's *aposematic*. A bright or distinctively contrasting aposematic color pattern—like the orange and black of the monarch butterfly or the black and white of a skunk—offers a warning to enemies that its bearer produces distasteful or harmful chemicals. (I have a theory about people and their various modes

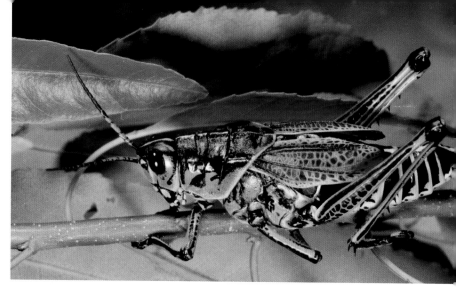

Though they eat widely, lubber grasshoppers are rarely pests.

of dress that relates to this concept, but I won't get into it here.) The contrasting coloration of the lubber grasshopper is definitely aposematic. Some birds get violently ill from eating a lubber, so the next time they see one, they "think twice" before pouncing. If you have ever stepped on one of these critters, you will remember the noxious odor that resulted. Lubbers will also use a menacing hiss to scare off would-be predators.

IMPACT Although lubbers will eat just about anything, their numbers rarely reach levels that cause serious economic damage for the homeowner. They are usually nothing more than a nuisance.

CONTROL Under normal circumstances, one can get rid of lubbers by hand. Because they are large, slow moving, and harmless to humans, a small net or a "smashing device" is sufficient to eliminate most problems within a few minutes. (A size 12 boot works nicely.) But sometimes large emergences do happen—and often in the same geographic area year after year. When pesticides are necessary, contact your local county agent for recommendations.

Dog-day Cicadas
The Original Summer Buzz

When I was growing up in central Virginia, my grandfather called them "jarflies" or "locusts," and their constant shrill, raspy calls were as much a part of summer as the long days, the heat, and the humidity. I spent many hot, lazy afternoons swimming in Blackwater Creek with my cousins Vernon and Earl as the cicadas' songs reverberated through the hardwood canopy that shaded the stream. When we were bored with the water, we would sometimes string the fearsome-looking cast larval skins on thread and wear them as "warrior" necklaces in one of our pretend worlds as native New Guinea tribesmen.

SCIENTIFIC NAMES Order Homoptera; Family Cicadidae; *Tibicen* spp.

The song of the adult male cicada is a summer serenade.

IDENTIFICATION The dog-day cicadas are aptly named because they are most active in the hot, humid "dog days" of late July and August. They call from early afternoon to dusk. Adults vary in size according to species, but many are rather large and robust insects, averaging about 2 inches in length. They have very large eyes on the sides of the head, and the body is often variously marked with brown, green, black, and white.

BIOLOGY Common dog-day cicadas have a life cycle that lasts 2–5 years. Because some of them emerge every year, they are also called "annual cicadas." (A close relative, the periodical cicada, has a life cycle of either 13 or 17 years and emerges in *large* numbers over relatively large geographical areas.) Females lay their eggs in clusters by "sawing" slits in twigs and small branches. The eggs hatch in 6–7 weeks, and the first-instar nymphs drop to the ground. The nymphs have large, muscular front legs made for digging. They immediately burrow into the soil, sometimes going several feet down, where they feed on tree roots. These little excavators live in their subterranean catacombs for 2–5 years. When fully developed, they emerge from the soil—almost always at night—through exit holes, often at the apex of a mud chimney as much as 3–4 inches tall. The nymph crawls up onto a nearby object, often the trunk of a tree. Its skin splits down the back, and the winged adult emerges, leaving the light brown shell attached to the tree trunk. The "cast skins" are easily recognizable and are very numerous in areas of heavy cicada activity. This adult emergence is believed to be the impetus for the ancient Chinese custom that holds cicadas as symbols of rebirth or immortality. Adults often live for 5–6 weeks.

The cicada "song" is made by the adult males, who "serenade" females with their repetitive refrain. The noise is produced by a pair of membranes, called tymbals, on the frontmost area of the "belly" that bend back and forth to produce a click. The individual "clicks" are produced so rapidly that the resulting noise is heard as a buzz and has been compared to the rough drone of a chain saw. The decibel level is about the same, too. Females are attracted by the racket, and mating ensues.

IMPACT Dog-day cicadas have very little economic significance. The females do occasional minor damage to limbs and twigs when they lay their eggs. Nymphal feeding on tree roots has little effect on trees and shrubs.

Lawn and Garden Insects

RELATIVES

Spider Mites

Nasty in Hot, Dry Weather

A graduate student of mine once jokingly referred to seemingly intelligent people who do stupid things as "running on the edge of the herd." His point was that as a part of natural selection, nature culls out the weak and incompetent by providing them as "food" for predators while more cunning competitors survive.

When summer days become hot and dry, and our busy schedules and occasional memory loss cause us to miss a watering or two, we may unwittingly force our plants to join those who "run on the edge of the herd." Dry summer conditions and other environmental factors may weaken plants, putting them under additional stress and making them very vulnerable to attack by some of their common enemies. Spider mites love hot, dry weather *and* plants under stress.

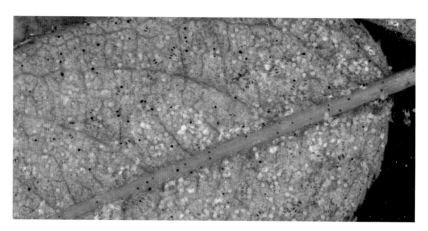

Spider mites can be serious pests in hot, dry weather.

SCIENTIFIC NAMES Order Acari; Family Tetranychidae

IDENTIFICATION Spider mites are not insects at all, but are more closely related to spiders and ticks. They have eight legs and a simple oval body without wings or antennae. To the naked eye, they may appear as tiny moving dots about the size of the period at the end of this sentence. However, they can be easily seen with a 10 x hand lens. Adult females are usually less than ½0 inch long, and a single colony may contain hundreds of individuals. The name "spider mite" comes from the silken webbing the mites produce on the underside of leaves. This webbing is an easy way to distinguish them from other kinds of mites.

BIOLOGY Mated females usually overwinter under bark or in litter or other debris. They emerge with the appearance of warm spring days and begin feeding and laying eggs. Spider mites can reproduce with alarming speed in hot weather. They are most troublesome from June through September. They thrive in hot, dusty conditions, and if everything is favorable can complete an entire generation in less than a week. They often first appear on plants adjacent to dusty roadways or on the edge of the garden. Plants under water stress are particularly susceptible. Heavy mite populations may suddenly crash in late summer from a variety of causes, usually some combination of predators, conditions more favorable for plants, cooler weather, and rain.

IMPACT Spider mites feed on a *wide* variety of ornamental plants and fruit trees. They have needlelike mouthparts and damage plants by sucking the fluids from individual plant cells, giving the leaves a stippled or flecked appearance. Heavy infestations may cause yellowing or bronzing of the leaves, which may drop prematurely. Severely damaged plants may be stunted or killed. The mites are usually found on the underside of leaves, but the damage may be most evident on the upper surface.

Spider Mites ·

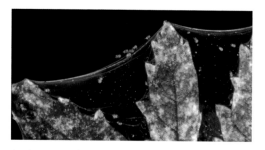
Spider mite webs can cover plant leaves.

The mites produce their fine silken webs from a pair of glands near the mouth, and the webs cover plant leaves, shoots, and flowers. When this webbing is very heavy, it may also shield the mites from pesticides.

CONTROL Spider mites are easiest to control when detected early. Two-spotted mites may hitchhike on purchased plants, so always inspect the lower leaf surfaces for evidence of mites before buying a plant. Spraying plants with a heavy stream of water can remove many mites from the leaves. The water spray should be directed upward against the underside of the leaves, and for this reason spraying works much better with smaller plants.

Spider mites have many natural enemies that can limit populations, including other predatory mites, thrips, ladybird beetles, and lacewing larvae. Adequate watering is important because water-stressed plants are much more susceptible. Watering pathways and other dusty areas may help to keep spider mite populations down.

Spider mites sometimes become a problem after the application of pesticides, because the insecticides kill the mites' natural enemies. Also, some pesticides seem to *stimulate* mite reproduction. Sevin, some organophosphates, and some pyrethroids seem to assist mite growth by increasing the amount of nitrogen in the host plant leaves. These insecticides applied during hot, dry weather may cause hefty increases within a few days. When pesticides are absolutely necessary, choices may include horticultural oils and insecticidal/miticidal soaps. You can contact your local county extension office for other recommendations.

Golden Garden Spiders

Welcome This Web Weaver to Feast in Your Garden

Fall means college football, cooler mornings, changing leaf colors, and—of course—big garden spiders in our shrubbery. Greek mythology named the spider after the Lydian princess Arachne, who challenged the goddess Athena to a weaving contest—and lost. As punishment Arachne was changed into a spider and condemned to spin forever. Every year, in early fall, I receive a number of queries about a beautiful yellow-and-black "Arachne" that has made a large orb web in someone's yard. Almost everyone wants to know if it is poisonous and a danger to humans.

A golden garden spider guards her egg sac.

SCIENTIFIC NAMES Order Arachnida; Family Argiopidae; *Argiope aurantia* Lucas

IDENTIFICATION The adult female golden garden spider, or writing spider, as this species is sometimes called, is about ¾ to 1 ⅛ inches long and spins a large web that may be 2 feet across. She has bright yellow or orange markings on a black background, and the cephalothorax, or upper part of the body, is covered with silvery hairs. Her long legs are mostly black, with some yellow or red markings close to the body. The adult male is much smaller, about ¼ to ⅜ inch long, and not as brightly colored. The male may build a much smaller web near that of the female.

Zigzag patterns reinforce webs.

BIOLOGY These beautiful creatures, like all arachnids, are predaceous and eat almost anything they can catch in their webs, which are strategically placed in high grass, across paths, between limbs of shrubbery, and sometimes even suspended across door or window frames. The web is a giant orb with guy lines radiating from the center like spokes on a wheel. The signature work of the garden spider's web, however, is a zigzag band of heavier white silk that extends down the center. This reinforcement is called a stabilimentum. The spider sits upside down in the center of the zigzag, waiting for an insect to become ensnared in her silken mesh. Anyone with a good imagination can envision actual writing in this heavier silk, hence the name "writing spider." Myth has it that those who see their name written in the spider silk will die soon. This web is *very* strong—sturdy enough to catch even the heavier flying insects, such as grasshoppers. When something flies into the sticky silk, the spider runs out and bites it, injecting a paralyzing venom, then quickly wraps it up in silk that she flings around it with her long hind legs. She then carries the prey back to the center of the web to consume at her leisure. Mating occurs in autumn, and the female produces a large silken cocoon that holds about a thousand tiny golden eggs. The spiderlings hatch within the cocoon and feed on each other until the following May, when the survivors emerge to begin the cycle anew.

IMPACT Although people are often very concerned about being bitten by these spiders, they are not considered dangerous. A large adult female may be capable of breaking the skin of a human, but the venom has not been shown to be harmful. Garden spiders are, in fact, very beneficial because they capture and feed on a number of insect pests that are ensnared in their webs.

Millipedes and Centipedes

Mainly Just a Nuisance

When I was a kid, we called them "hundred-leggers" and "thousand-leggers." We would find them while turning over stones or sifting through rotting logs just to see what was under there. They were easy to tell apart. The centipedes, or "hundred-legged worms," galloped across the ground like tiny racehorses, while the millipedes, or "thousand-legged worms," moved with the determination and swiftness of a medicated sloth.

SCIENTIFIC NAMES Millipedes: Order Diplopoda; Centipedes: Order Chilopoda

IDENTIFICATION Centipedes and millipedes are not insects, but are related more closely to shrimp, crayfish, and lobsters. Both have long, many-segmented bodies with distinct heads. Centipedes are yellowish to brownish, flattened top to bottom, and have a pair of long antennae. Millipedes are often brown to blackish, more rounded, and have a pair of short antennae. Centipedes have a pair of poison claws behind the head (these look like mouthparts) that they use to paralyze the small insects, spiders, and other small animals on which they feed. In Georgia, centipedes range in length from 1 to 3 inches.

Centipedes can bite.

BIOLOGY Centipedes occupy a variety of habitats but prefer dark, moist sites beneath stones, woodpiles, leaves, and bark. An exception is the "house centipede," which can adapt well to the inside of homes and lives in basements, damp closets, and bathrooms. This species is grayish

Millipedes are slow moving and prefer moist environments.

yellow with three long stripes on its back. It has fifteen pairs of very long legs, and in the female, the last pair is more than twice the body length. Though house centipedes are only an inch or so long, their long legs make them look much larger. They move *very* quickly when disturbed, can climb walls easily, and are sometimes mistaken for long-legged spiders. House centipedes are usually active at night, when they seek out roaches and other small insects. If house centipedes are plentiful in your home, a moisture problem is indicated.

Millipedes vary in length from less than an inch to more than 2 inches. They are scavengers, preferring decaying organic matter like leaves, mulch, piles of wood, and other decomposing material. When disturbed, they will sometimes curl up like pillbugs. Millipedes also prefer moist environments. Sometimes they migrate in large numbers, especially in the cooler days of fall or after heavy rains. It is during these times that they may invade homes. Because they crawl along on the ground, the basement and first floor are the primary areas of infestation. They climb walls easily and can enter through any small opening. Most die from desiccation soon after they come inside.

IMPACT Some of the larger centipedes can bite, and the result is usually a reaction similar to a mild bee sting. Only individuals who have a heightened sensitivity to arthropod poisons are in any real danger. Millipedes are not poisonous but can produce an irritating, foul-smelling fluid that may cause an allergic reaction in some people. In some species, this chemical, used as a defense mechanism, contains cyanide. Always wash your hands after handling a millipede. Centipedes and millipedes occasionally become nuisance pests in homes. Neither carries serious diseases, nor do they damage food or other belongings in the home.

CONTROL Several practices will help to keep centipede and millipede populations in check.

- Remove preferred environments outside the home. Eliminate rocks, boards, woodpiles, mulch, and similar accumulations from the area around the house.
- Dethatch the lawn and mow closely to promote drier conditions and repel these pests. Watering in the morning rather than the evening will allow the lawn to dry before they become active at night.
- Exclude them from entering your home by caulking all cracks and crevices, and make sure all doors and windows fit tightly.
- If millipedes and centipedes occur in large numbers, an insecticide treatment may be in order. Sprays or dusts of various materials (contact your local county extension office for recommendations) applied around the foundation, doors, and windows will provide temporary control. You may also apply liquid or granular forms to mulched flower beds and heavily thatched turf. When treating inside, treat cracks and crevices along baseboards and other places where they have been seen in larger numbers.

Chiggers
Ooooohhh, Those Itchy Redbugs!

Few creatures can cause as much discomfort and misery for their size as the tiny chigger can. From midsummer through early fall, chiggers can turn a pleasant outdoor activity into an unpleasant and irritating experience that may seem to last forever. Chiggers are not insects. They are the larval stage of the common red harvest mite. These little demons play havoc with hikers, fishermen, campers, picnickers, birdwatchers, berry gatherers, and homeowners who venture into woodlands, berry patches, orchards, and open fields. They can even become a nuisance in mown lawns if the conditions are shady and moist. Chiggers are most numerous when the vegetation is heavy and damp. The worst chigger attack that I have personally

Chigger bites inject digestive enzymes, causing itching and swelling.

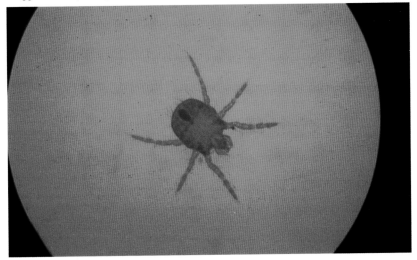

experienced followed a hike through high grass in an uncut pasture—with no protection from repellents—while wearing shorts. Within a few hours, both legs were covered from ankle to thigh with what seemed like hundreds of chigger bites. The resulting discomfort is something that I will never forget.

SCIENTIFIC NAMES Order Acari; Family Trombiculidae; *Trombicula alfreddu-gesi* (Oudemans)

BIOLOGY In the spring, the eight-legged red harvest mite lays up to fifteen eggs per day in leaf litter, damp soil, or overgrown weeds. The eggs hatch in about a week, and the emerging six-legged "chiggers," only about $\frac{1}{128}$ of an inch long and hungry for a meal, crawl up onto the tips of nearby vegetation and wait in ambush to snag a passing host. They are attracted to carbon dioxide and attach to any warm-blooded animal that exhales, from field mice to humans. Once on a suitable host, they wander around a bit before settling down to feed. On humans, they prefer an area where clothing is tight—favorite places are around the waistline and under socks—or where the skin is thin and tender, like the armpits, ankles, the bend of the elbows and knees, or the groin.

IMPACT Contrary to popular belief, chiggers do not burrow into the skin. Instead, they pierce the skin with their mouthparts and inject saliva containing powerful digestive enzymes that break down skin cells. These enzymes also cause the local tissues to swell and harden. The tiny chigger sits within this swollen tissue, sucking up its liquefied meal. After about 4 days, it drops from the host, leaving behind a red welt with a hard white center *and* a sadistic itch. The welts, itching, and swelling occur within 3–6 hours after exposure and may last up to 2 weeks. Some people experience more severe allergic reactions and may also develop blisterlike lesions. Persistent scratching—and it's hard to do anything else—may lead to infection.

CONTROL The preventive measures listed below can be very effective and are *strongly* recommended.

- When possible, avoid walking through overgrown vegetation, uncut fields, and brush.
- Always apply a repellent to shoes, socks, cuffs, the waistline, and pant legs. Products that contain DEET or permethrin are effective.
- Wear long pants tucked into boots or socks when hiking or camping in chigger-infested areas.
- Mow grass, weeds, and thick vegetation to remove chigger habitats close to your home.
- Because chiggers usually move around for a while before they attach, you should always launder field clothes in hot water immediately after returning from a chigger-infested area and take a hot bath to remove chiggers that have not yet settled in. If itching persists (the stylostomes, or mouthparts, often remain in the skin), apply ointments containing benzocaine, hydrocortisone, or calamine lotion.

Ticks

Don't Get "Ticked" with Warm Spring Weather

If you saw the 1993 movie *Ticks*, you had far too much time on your hands. If you missed it, gigantic ticks developed as a result of steroid sprays applied to marijuana plants and siphoned the body fluids from teens camping in Northern California. Does this general storyline sound familiar? People have always loathed ticks. And why not? They suck blood for a living and carry pathogens that make people sick. Just the thought of them gives me a nervous tic, and *that* really ticks me off.

SCIENTIFIC NAMES Order Acari; Family Ixodidae; *Amblyomma americanum* (Linnaeus), *Dermacentor variabilis* (Say), *Ixodes scapularis* Say

IDENTIFICATION Ticks are arachnids, and thus are more closely related to spiders than to insects. They have eight legs and a fused cephalothorax and abdomen. Engorged female ticks are three to ten times larger than their unfed counterparts. Three tick species are very common in Georgia: the Lone Star tick has a white spot in the middle of its back; the American dog tick has a lighter area directly behind the head (but not a "spot"); and the black-legged tick, or deer tick, is dark brown with no light markings.

BIOLOGY Ticks are blood-feeding external parasites of reptiles, birds, and mammals, including humans. They are also important vectors of disease, including but not limited to Lyme disease, Rocky Mountain spotted fever, and tularemia. Ticks become active with the warm days of spring. They generally have a three-stage life cycle, progressing from egg to larva to nymph to adult. Most species have different hosts for each stage. Ticks lay eggs in various places, but never on their host. The young, sometimes called

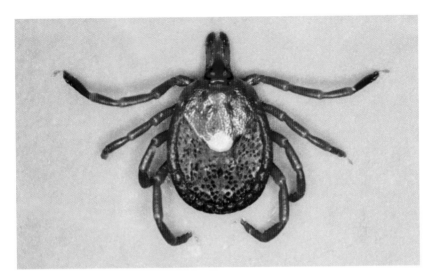

The Lone Star tick is a vector of Rocky Mountain spotted fever.

"seed ticks," seek out a host for a blood meal, then usually drop off to molt. They generally prefer overgrown vegetation—vacant lots, fields, the edges of trails, weedy roadsides, and underbrush along creeks and rivers near animal nesting or bedding areas. They climb up onto the tips of grass and weeds and wait for a suitable host to brush against them.

IMPACT Ticks inject saliva into their host as they feed, sometimes transmitting disease along with it. The American dog tick and Lone Star tick transmit Rocky Mountain spotted fever and tularemia, while the black-legged tick carries Lyme disease. Tick paralysis can result when an engorging female tick transmits a neurotoxin from her salivary glands into the host. The tick usually has to be attached for several days for symptoms to occur. These include fatigue, muscle pain, and numbness in the legs. Paralysis moves rapidly upward from the legs to the arms, and eventually to the tongue and face. Extreme cases may exhibit convulsions and respiratory failure. Tick

REMOVING TICKS

Use a pair of forceps, grasp the tick as close to the head as possible and pull upward with slowly increasing pressure. Do *not* jerk the tick or squeeze its body. You may break off the mouthparts or actually inject the tick's body contents into your body, and infection could result. If you have difficulty removing the mouthparts, seek the assistance of a healthcare provider.

paralysis is sometimes confused with Guillain-Barré syndrome, botulism, and myasthenia gravis. The paralysis usually stops once the tick has been removed; however, the condition can be fatal if the source of the problem is not found. Fortunately, human cases are rare. They usually occur in children younger than ten.

CONTROL You can take several precautions to help minimize the impact of ticks.

- Keep weeds to a minimum and keep your lawn closely mown. Ticks do not do well in open sunshine.
- When hiking, keep your pant cuffs tucked into your socks.
- Walk in the middle of trails to avoid brushing vegetation.
- Wear DEET or some other insect repellent.
- Examine yourself for ticks immediately on returning home. (If you are camping, do this *every* evening.)
- Remove ticks as soon as you find them. The quicker you remove them, the less chance there is of contagion.

Household Insects

Bedbugs and Batbugs

Tiny Bedroom Vampires

"Creatures of the night, they emerge from their dark retreats and creep silently over the bed, ever watchful of the sleepers wrestling fitfully with their dreams. The bodies are warm, the creatures' need for blood is great, and soon piercing mouths press tender skin as they hungrily begin to feed." If you think this reads like an excerpt from a poorly written vampire novel, think again. It's an accurate description of the activities of bedbugs and batbugs after they have become established in your home.

Bedbugs feed while we sleep.

And infestations are on the increase across the country. Once the scourge of cheap, seedy hotels, bedbugs and batbugs are now being found in more upscale establishments.

SCIENTIFIC NAMES Order Hemiptera; Family Cimicidae; Common bedbug: *Cimex lectularis* Linnaeus; Batbug: *Cimex adjunctus* Barber

IDENTIFICATION Bedbugs and batbugs are wingless insects with oval, flattened bodies. When unfed, they are about ¼ inch long, brownish in color, and have a shriveled upper surface like a dried prune. A well-fed bedbug looks like a completely different insect. The body swells, elongates, and changes color to a dull reddish black after a large blood meal. Eggs are white and tiny, about 1/32 inch long. Newly hatched individuals are translucent and nearly colorless, but otherwise they look much like the adults. These insects emit an oily liquid that has a distinctive obnoxious odor. Their presence can easily be determined by that smell alone if the numbers are high enough.

BIOLOGY One adult female can lay up to two hundred eggs, and when fed regularly can deposit them at a rate of three to four per day in the cracks and crevices in which the adults hide. There may be as many as three or four generations a year. At first, bedbugs may be found only along the seams, tufts, and folds in mattresses and covers, but if left untreated they will spread to crevices in the bedsteads, baseboards, window casings, pictures, and furniture; behind loose wallpaper; and in other hidden spots. Batbugs, as the name implies, are normally found on bats. They begin their house infestation in the attic—or wherever the bat population exists—but they will move down to the bedroom if their natural hosts are removed. They are quite comfortable in the niche formerly claimed only by bedbugs and can exist there for long periods.

IMPACT Hiding places are often marked by black or brown excrement spots on the surfaces where the insects rest, and their unmistakable odor can become unpleasant when their numbers become very high. These creatures usually feed at night, biting people while they sleep. If their hunger becomes too great and the light is dim, however, they will steal from their wallpaper coffins, dodging direct sun rays, and move silently across the covers to their unsuspecting prey. (I wonder if Count Dracula kept them as pets.) These insects inject toxic saliva into the skin as they feed to facilitate the process. Though the bite itself is often painless, the saliva causes welts and itching. Fecal smears and blood spots are often visible on sheets, mattresses, and pillow cases. There are no known associations with disease transmission, and the only medical consequences relate to the itching and welts.

Why have bedbugs and batbugs suddenly become a problem in homes?

- Pest control specialists cite increased tourism from abroad. These little blood-sucking vagabonds will readily hitch a ride in luggage, laundry, or furniture, then move out to the first warm sleeping body when their journey is complete.
- Many of the older products that worked to eliminate this pest—like DDT, chlordane, and other pesticides—are no longer available.
- Possible insecticide resistance has been reported, perhaps facilitated by the increased use of less toxic insect baits and growth regulators for other pests.
- Bedbugs can go for up to 6 months without feeding.

CONTROL Locate and treat all cracks and crevices where bedbugs and bat-bugs may be hiding. When inspecting for infestations, look both for the insects and for the distinctive blood spots and fecal stains that suggest a nearby hiding place. Pesticides of choice include cyfluthrin, deltamethrin, and pyrethrins plus synergist. *Never* treat bed linens with pesticides. Mattresses should be treated *only* along seams, tufts, and buttons. Locate and eliminate potential wild animal sources, including bats, birds, and squirrels, from the walls and attic of the home. If insects are found in these areas, insecticides should be applied. When using pesticides, *always* follow the directions on the label.

Finally, if you are careful and have a steady hand, you may also use *very tiny* wooden stakes.

Moth Flies

Unwanted Guests in Your Drains

You may well be entertaining overnight guests—unwanted guests. In fact, they may have been staying with you for some time now without your knowledge, crawling in the labyrinths that wind their way round and round through the pipes connecting your sinks and showers to the main sewage lines. Their maggot-like larvae feed quietly out of sight, slithering around in the rotting vegetation, slowly growing fat and hardy on the fungi, algae, and other microorganisms inhabiting the accumulated slime. Soon they will pupate, and when the hairy-winged adults emerge, they will eagerly move upward to the light. It's an *X-Files* exclusive: "The Invasion of the Moth Flies, coming soon to a drain near you."

Moth flies live in the decaying material down in our drains.

SCIENTIFIC NAMES Order Diptera; Family Psychodidae; *Psychoda* sp.

IDENTIFICATION Moth flies, or drain flies, are common, though often over-looked, insects associated with drain pipes and related moist areas. There are many species. Adults may be yellow to brown to black and vary in length from ⅟₁₆ to ¼ inch. Tiny hairs cover the body and wings, and because they hold their wings rooflike over their bodies when at rest, they look like very tiny moths. The adults usually occur in very small numbers, flitting around our sinks like tiny hairy gnats.

BIOLOGY Eggs, larvae, and pupae can be found in the gelatinous film, muck, and slime of drains, overflow pipes, septic tanks, and similar places. They may even develop in dirty garbage cans, tree holes, and rain barrels. Eggs laid on these moist media hatch in 1½ to 2 days, and the emerging immature maggots feed for about 2 weeks. The larvae are actually consid-ered beneficial because they break down drain wastes into water-soluble compounds. They pupate on the surface of this grunge, and adults emerge 20–40 hours later. The entire life cycle can be completed in 1–3 weeks, with the time depending on the temperature.

IMPACT Moth flies in small numbers are not a problem, and many home-owners tolerate them, often without giving them a second look. But they can appear in large numbers — suddenly and without warning — and cause a nuisance around homes and sewage treatment facilities. Adults swarm around lampshades at night and get in windows, tubs, showers, and drains. Outdoors they may get in eyes, ears, and noses, and their feces can mar fresh paint. Inhaling fragments and dust of dead flies may cause problems for people with bronchial asthma. Because these flies develop in filth, dis-ease transmission is always a possibility.

CONTROL The adults are not strong fliers, and aerosol or spray insecticides will easily kill them. But for long-term control, the breeding sites must be found and the fly's life cycle disrupted. Drain cleaners like Drano remove organic matter from drains and traps. If this is not successful, mechanical cleaning with a stiff, long-handled brush may be necessary to remove any remaining film. If the flies continue to be a problem, consult a pest control operator. Broken pipes or other moisture problems that are not readily visible may be the primary source of the infestation. Before hiring any professional, consider getting quotes from two or three firms.

Fruit Flies

Drunk on Their Own Success

When I think of fruit flies, I am reminded of this verse:

DRUNKARDS (VINEGAR FLIES)

They float and bob and weave and dance
as if in an eternal trance.
A rotten peach is their salvation,
coaxing their intoxication.

—*Anonymous*

All of us have seen the swarms of little flies that float above our fruit or vegetable bowls, doing an aerial stagger that would eclipse the rambling stroll of even the most ardent dipsomaniac. They are also called vinegar flies and drunkards. The latter name is very fitting because they feed exclusively on the liquids from fermentation. One writer has even suggested that the reason their flight is so erratic is because they live in an eternal state of inebriation. Fruit flies can be a problem year-round for those who keep bowls of fresh fruit and vegetables on counters as functional kitchen décor.

SCIENTIFIC NAMES Order Diptera; Family Drosophilidae; *Drosophila* sp.

IDENTIFICATION Fruit flies are very tiny—about ⅛ inch long—and often have red eyes. Their bodies usually appear tan in front and black behind. Their erratic flight patterns in the vicinity of spoiling fruit are usually a dead giveaway.

BIOLOGY Adult females lay their eggs on the surface of fermenting foods, and the emerging larvae continue to feed there. The reproductive potential

Fruit flies can go through an entire life cycle in about a week.

of fruit flies is gigantic. If left undisturbed, females may lay as many as five hundred eggs, and the entire life cycle can take place within a week.

IMPACT These little floating drunkards are common in our homes, in restaurants, in markets, and any other place where food is allowed to decay and ferment. Apples, peaches, bananas, tomatoes, melons, squash, grapes, and other perishable items from the garden are the usual source of indoor infestations. But though they are attracted to ripening fruits and vegetables, fruit flies may also breed in garbage disposals, drains, trash containers, and empty cans. They have even been known to develop in wet mops! All they need is a moist film on some fermenting substance. They are often brought into the home on fruits and vegetables that were previously infested, but they can also enter through poorly screened doors or windows. Though fruit flies are primarily nuisance pests, they can contaminate food with bacteria and other disease-producing organisms. Their presence in large numbers can be a source of major frustration for the homeowner.

Fruit flies feed on fermenting fruits and vegetables.

CONTROL Once a home has been infested with fruit flies, it is necessary to find and eliminate all breeding areas. Fail to do so and the problem will continue regardless of any attempts to control the adults. One sometimes has to be very creative to find all of these sites. To determine if the flies are in the garbage disposal or drain, tape a clear plastic bag over the opening overnight. If flies are present, the adults will emerge and be trapped in the bag the next morning. After locating the breeding sites, construct a simple trap by placing a paper funnel (from a rolled sheet of paper) into a small jar primed with a few ounces of cider vinegar (or a small slice of banana). The remaining flies will enter the funnel and become trapped inside.

Prevention involves good sanitation. Eliminate sources of attraction. Ripe fruit and produce should be eaten, thrown away, or refrigerated. Damaged pieces should be removed and discarded. A single piece of fruit left in the back of the closet, or fruit juice spilled beneath the cabinet or refrigerator, may be the source of thousands of flies. Windows and doors should have tight-fitting screens (16 mesh) to keep adult flies from entering homes.

Cluster Flies

They Only Seem like a Serious Problem

You're sitting at home on a warm winter evening, kicked back, feet up, sipping a glass of merlot and watching a *Forensic Files* rerun. You know the one: a body has just been found in an abandoned farmhouse, and investigators are met at the door by a swarm of blue and green flies. Suddenly your son cries out: "Dad, what are all these flies doing around the upstairs window?" You run upstairs, and sure enough—the window is literally crawling with slow-moving, relatively large gray flies. You look at the door leading back into the attic, and there are flies resting near the door handle. Where did they come from? You have no fly problems outside. In fact, you haven't even *seen* a fly in several weeks—until now. Suddenly, you're paranoid about

Cluster flies are slow moving and are often found on windowsills.

what's behind that attic door. The good news is that this culprit is not a harbinger of dead bodies or any other vermin in the recesses of your attic walls. It's only the cluster fly.

SCIENTIFIC NAMES Order Diptera; Family Calliphoridae; *Pollenia rudis* (Fabricius)

IDENTIFICATION Cluster flies are slightly larger than house flies and are dark gray. The thorax of newly emerged adults is covered with golden hairs, or setae, and when the fly is at rest the wings overlap slightly at the tips. House flies, in contrast, spread their wings slightly when at rest. The common name comes from the flies' habit of entering buildings and gathering in clusters. Cluster flies muddle around windows and lights, moving slowly and bumping into objects in their path. They also have the distinctive habit of falling to the floor and spinning noisily on their backs until they're exhausted. It puts an entirely new spin on the word *flywheel*.

BIOLOGY In early spring, adult females that have survived the winter deposit their eggs in cracks in the soil. The larvae burrow into the ground and parasitize earthworms. Total development time varies from 27 to 39 days, depending on temperature and other factors. There are about four generations a year, and the adults are found in fields during the summer, not in houses. When the temperature drops in the fall, the flies move toward shelters, often settling on south- or southwest-facing walls or roofs. As the day cools, the flies enter cracks and crevices on the exterior of the building and settle down for the winter. On warm days they break their dormancy and move around. This movement invariably takes some of them inside. They are strongly attracted to light. When cluster flies are crushed, they give off a sweet odor. This smell is detectable when they gather in large clusters and may act as an attractant for other flies.

IMPACT The cluster fly is a pest of homes, schools, and office buildings. The flies are strictly a nuisance pest and do not bite or carry disease.

CONTROL Houses that are surrounded by large shade trees rarely have a problem, presumably because the earthworms the larvae parasitize don't live beneath these trees.

Caulking any openings to the interior — windows, doors, screening, vents, and so on — is important, but often it is virtually impossible to "screen them out." When the flies become active inside, you can spray with an aerosol containing pyrethrins to kill those in the vicinity. You can also add to your aerobics workout by swinging a fly swatter at the ones you see on the sill. Remember how much fun you had as a kid pretending you were the hero in the Brothers Grimm fairy tale "Seven with One Blow"? Try it again. You'll certainly get more exercise with that swatter than you would sitting on the sofa watching *Forensic Files.*

Cockroaches
Will They Outlast Us All?

"La cucaracha, la cucaracha, ya no puede caminar." Many of us can still sing or hum the first few lines of this well-known children's song. But this jingle in any form is the last thing on our minds when we discover these detestable creatures in our home. Cockroaches have been around for more than 300 million years and have changed relatively little during that time compared with other organisms. They are incredibly adaptable and have adjusted well to living with humans.

In Georgia there are five or so important species that invade houses; the two discussed here are lumped together in a small group commonly referred to as "palmetto bugs." Somehow, it seems a bit more socially acceptable to say that we have "palmetto bugs" rather than "roaches." The effect of the presence of a large cockroach, physically harmless though it may be, should not be underestimated. I have actually seen adults scream and run from the room when confronted with a large palmetto bug. I remember one particular evening when we were visiting friends and a large adult flew into the room and landed on the back of our hostess's neck. The result, had it been on tape, would have been the big winner on *America's Funniest Videos.*

SCIENTIFIC NAMES Order Blattaria; Family Blattidae; American cockroach: *Periplaneta americana* (Linnaeus); Smoky brown cockroach: *Periplaneta fuliginosa* (Serville)

IDENTIFICATION The American cockroach and the smoky brown cockroach are similar in general appearance and biology. The adult American roach is 1½ to 2 inches long, reddish brown, and has pale "halolike" markings

Cockroaches have been around for 300 million years.

behind the head. The smaller smoky brown is 1 to 1½ inches in length and uniformly "smoky brown" in color. Both can live outdoors and are often self-prescribed caretakers of that dark and clammy space beneath decks, porches, and crawl spaces.

BIOLOGY Both species produce a small egg case called an ootheca in which about sixteen to twenty eggs are deposited. Females drop these cases in secluded places and the eggs hatch in about 6 weeks. The young reach adulthood in another 6–12 months. When disturbed, palmetto bugs can run *very* rapidly, but on rare occasions the adults may fly as well. Though they prefer areas of higher moisture, palmetto bugs can be found anywhere in the house, at least on the first floor. They enter homes whenever and wherever opportunity permits, through an open door or window or any tiny crevice that affords an entrance.

IMPACT Their presence alone is enough to afford them "pest status" (especially when they land abruptly on your neck), but in addition palmetto bugs feed on a wide variety of plant and animal material. Roaches can contaminate food; damage books, clothing, and wallpaper; and in large numbers can produce a very unpleasant odor. They have even been associated with childhood asthma.

CONTROL Though generally not present in large numbers, these pests will move inside during certain times of year, especially in the fall when outdoor temperatures are cooling down. Exclusion is one way to slow down this seasonal invasion. Seal outside doors with weather stripping. Use caulking compounds for gaps in walls and floors where pipes enter. Basement populations can be reduced by controlling dampness with dehumidifiers. If roaches have established a population inside, keep food and garbage sealed in tight containers. Keep clutter from accumulating, and vacuum often. Good sanitation is imperative both inside *and* outside the house.

If chemical control becomes necessary, there are many products on the market today for roach control. Most come in spray, dust, or bait form. Though sprays offer the quickest control, they may also repel roaches, and those that survive the initial kill will simply hide until the pesticide residue has diminished. Dusts are longer lasting. Boric acid is perhaps the most popular and can be very effective when applied in a thin film in out-of-the-way places — under refrigerators, stoves, sinks, and in wall voids. Baits can be extremely effective, but remember to use the larger bait stations for palmetto bugs!

German Cockroaches

Small Insects, Big Problems

I'm sure you've heard it said that in the event of a nuclear war, the one sure survivor would be the cockroach. There is ample evidence to support that ominous claim. Cockroaches have been around, in almost the same form, for more than 300 million years. They are incredibly adaptable and are more than happy to live with humans. Of the five or so roach species that invade homes in Georgia, the German roach is arguably the most persistent and the most difficult to control. The first house I ever purchased had a resident population that I was unaware of for several months. Then it exploded.

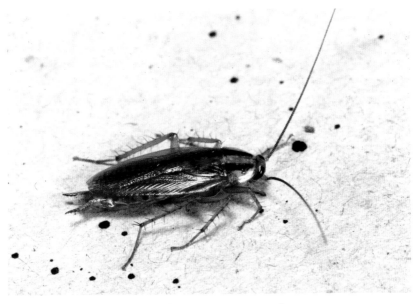

German roaches are major pests of homes, restaurants, and apartments.

I remember well going into the kitchen at two o'clock in the morning, rolled up newspaper in hand, flipping on the light, and flailing wildly at the skittering horde of roaches as they dashed for the cover.

SCIENTIFIC NAMES Order Blattaria; Family Blattellidae; *Blattella germanica* (Linnaeus)

IDENTIFICATION German cockroaches have a flattened, oval body; spiny legs; and long, filamentous antennae. Adults are light tan to medium brown with two dark stripes (separated by a lighter stripe) on the shield directly behind the head, and are ½ to ⅝ inch long. Although they have wings that cover the entire abdomen, they rarely fly. Young roaches are wingless and nearly black with a light stripe separating two darker bands running about halfway down the middle of the back. The egg capsules are light tan and usually less than ¼ inch long.

BIOLOGY Unlike most other roaches, the female German cockroach carries her ootheca, or egg capsule, protruding from her abdomen until the eggs are ready to hatch. Then she drops the capsule in a quiet location and the nymphs emerge. It usually takes about 4 weeks for the capsule to hatch from the time it begins to form. She may produce as many as four to eight capsules, about one every 6 weeks, each with two to three dozen eggs. Assuming two generations a year, one adult female can produce more than ten thousand descendants.

IMPACT German cockroaches are a general nuisance, and their very presence in a home is enough to generate alarm and discomfort. They also produce smelly secretions that can affect the flavor of various foods. When populations are high, this smell can be detected in the general area of the infestation. Disease organisms have been found on roach bodies, and the possibility exists for manual transmission of these organisms by roaches.

The cast skins and excrement also contain various allergens that can produce watery eyes, sneezing, congestion, asthma, and skin rashes.

CONTROL It is almost impossible to keep cockroaches from coming inside the house. They commonly enter in grocery bags, boxes, suitcases, and in a hundred other ways. But good sanitation practices will prevent serious problems. Keep the kitchen clean of spilled foods, including crumbs on the floor. Do not leave dirty dishes out overnight. Vacuum often. Empty the garbage every night into a tightly sealed container. Structural modifications may also be in order. Be sure holes in walls where pipes pass through the kitchen and bathroom are well caulked.

There are several options when chemical control becomes necessary. Dusts are slow acting but give long-lasting control. Of these, boric acid is the most commonly used and can be very effective. It should be applied in a thin film in out-of-the-way places such as beneath sinks, stoves, refrigerators, washers and dryers, and in wall voids. Baits can also be very effective. They usually come in a gel tube or paper/plastic stations. Among those recommended for Georgia are amindinohydrazone (Maxforce, Combat), orthobotric acid, and hydramethylnon. Other contact insecticides are available, but these often repel roaches as much as they control them. *Always follow the label carefully when using pesticides.*

Oriental Cockroaches

Nasty Nuisances

Greasy, grungy, nasty, filthy, grubby, gross. All these words — and more — have been commonly used to describe one of our more frequent uninvited house guests: *roaches.* I have already discussed the American and German cockroaches, so in the interest of ethnic fair play, this chapter's topic is the Oriental cockroach. In case you are wondering, this insect has no special affinity for rice or shark fin soup, any more than the American roach leaps with delight onto a plate of country fried chicken or the German roach to Wiener schnitzel.

Oriental roaches are often deemed the dirtiest of our house infestants.

SCIENTIFIC NAMES Order Blattaria; Family Blattidae; *Blatta orientalis* (Linnaeus)

IDENTIFICATION Adult Oriental cockroaches are about 1 to 1¼ inches long, shiny, dark brown to black, and lack functional wings. Females have two small wing pads, and the slightly smaller males have wings that do not reach the tip of the abdomen. The egg case is dark reddish brown, about an inch long (the longest of our common house-infesting species), and appears slightly inflated, like an elongate balloon.

BIOLOGY Outside, this insect occurs in leaf litter and other debris. Indoors, however, its common name, "water bug," comes from its close association with damp areas—much more so than other roach species. Because they feed on decaying organic matter and garbage, Oriental cockroaches are often considered the filthiest of the house-infesting species. They occur within wall spaces, crawl spaces, basements, and drains. They may crawl along water pipes to get from floor to floor. Females often deposit their egg cases onto a surface that is warm and protected and near a food source. An adult female can produce about eight capsules, each containing about sixteen eggs, in her lifetime. Development is slow and may take up to 20 months at room temperature from egg to adult. Adults live 1–6 months.

IMPACT These pests, like their American and German cousins, are primarily a nuisance, and because they feed on filth they have often been accused of being disease vectors. In addition, this species has an offensive odor when present in large numbers.

CONTROL Sanitation is extremely important. The removal of food, moisture, and harborages for these pests is the first step in their control. This includes caulking cracks in cabinets and closets, and beneath sinks in the kitchen and bathroom (the two rooms where this insect is found most often).

Silica gel, boric acid, and diatomaceous earth are all effective chemical measures if applied to cracks and crevices and other wall voids. These dusts should be used lightly, and never in damp areas. Baits can be effective as well, including bait stations, gels, and pastes. Other space sprays and aerosols are available, but some of these can be applied only by a licensed pest control operator.

Booklice

Tiny Bibliophiles

You may not know it, but there are strangers in your library—or in the basement or the attic. Their name might sound a bit pedagogical, but they're certainly not snobs. In fact, they're really quite "down to earth." They enjoy rummaging through old books and magazines, in boxes at estate sales, in attics and basements, and, yes, even in forgotten corners of our home. They're a bit shy, so you may not have seen them. But you've certainly seen the signs of their presence: loose pages, some with ragged holes, in old books; book covers that fell away on lifting them from the box (or from the shelf). Such damage is often the result of a booklouse infestation (not to be confused with a "bookworm," who would *never* intentionally damage a piece of reading material).

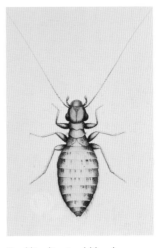

Booklice live in old books.

SCIENTIFIC NAMES Order Psocoptera; Family Psocidae

IDENTIFICATION Booklice are tiny, soft-bodied insects that range in length from about ¹⁄₃₂ to ³⁄₁₆ inch and appear transparent to grayish white. They are usually wingless and may go unnoticed unless their numbers are extremely high. Their outdoor relatives include the barklice.

BIOLOGY Most booklice are females that reproduce by parthenogenesis (development from unfertilized eggs). Each adult female deposits sixty or so tiny white oval eggs near a food source, either singly or in clusters, and when the nymphs hatch they immediately begin feeding on molds and mildews. Time from egg to adult varies from 1 to 2 months, depending on environmental conditions. These little eating machines prefer dark, moist habitats with temperatures between 75 and 85 degrees. Outbreaks often follow long periods of humid, warm weather.

IMPACT Contrary to some reports, booklice *do not* bite humans or animals (though skin irritation is a rare consequence for highly sensitive individuals), nor do they spread disease. Though booklice prefer molds and fungi, these tiny critters eat a variety of other things, including book bindings, glue, photographs, wallpaper, cereals, flour, pollen, dead insect fragments, bird nests, and certain house plants. Usually, their numbers are not high enough to cause significant damage, but occasionally an outbreak will require some kind of control program.

CONTROL Reduce moisture to reduce or eliminate mold formation. Locate and remove breeding sites, such as damp books or other papers, mattresses, moldy wood, upholstered furniture, and damp foodstuffs. If these items are salvageable, dry them in direct sunlight. Open doors to ventilate and dry infested areas, or expedite the procedure with a dehumidifier or fan. Seal other foodstuffs in moisture-proof containers. Store books and anything else made of paper off the floor. Fix plumbing leaks and drain leaks to eliminate moisture sources. Other moisture control procedures can be done as necessary.

Usually, no chemical control is necessary because damage to commodities is negligible. When booklice are present in large numbers and additional measures are required, aerosol cans containing pyrethrins can be used to spray the bugs directly as well as their habitats. When using pesticides *always* read and follow the directions on the label.

Carpet Beetles

Another Personal Horror Movie

One of my passions away from the "office" is horror fiction and films. Perhaps that's the reason I have always found insects so appealing: they're naturals as subject matter. I *love* horror films like *The Wasp Woman, The Fly, Arachnophobia, Mimic,* and *Blue Monkey.* And sometimes, when I find myself with an insect problem that seems out of hand, I feel as if I'm in the middle of my own personal horror flick. There is a good reason why insects have such a great potential to terrorize. Insect pests have been a blight on humankind since before recorded history. They feed on virtually *everything* humans consider valuable: their homes, their foods, their clothing, and

Carpet beetle larvae feed on a variety of plant and animal products.

even their bodies. Imagine this fictional scenario: a family is sleeping all snug in their beds, and suddenly a tiny, spiny creature slithers out from the very walls of the house and feeds hungrily on all the possessions they hold dear. Wait. That's reality, not fiction.

SCIENTIFIC NAMES Order Coleoptera; Family Dermestidae

IDENTIFICATION Carpet beetles are semiomnivorous feeders (that means they will eat almost anything) that attack numerous commodities. Several species specialize in household goods. Adults are usually ⅛ to ³⁄₁₆ inch in length, and they come in a variety of colors. One is shiny black; others have brightly colored patterns of white, brown, yellow, and orange. The larvae are about ¼ inch long and are densely covered with hairs. Only the larvae damage our possessions.

BIOLOGY Adults live outside and feed on a wide variety of flowers. They gain access to homes through open windows or any other slight opening. They seek out susceptible fabrics and other materials and lay their eggs on them. The eggs hatch in 1 ½ to 2 weeks, and the larvae feed on the animal-based products until they pupate. The larval stage lasts from 6 weeks to 6 months, depending on heat, moisture, and the availability of food. Adults emerge in a few days to a few weeks.

IMPACT Carpet beetle larvae eat a wide variety of animal and plant substances, including hides, fur, feathers, wool, silk, felt, horns, and bone, as well as cereals, grains, red pepper, meal and flour, powdered milk, pet foods, leather, book bindings, dead insects, bird and animal nests, and even rayon and linens. Very little in our home is safe once they get started. The larvae prefer to feed in dark, quiet areas like closets, attics, inside boxes of stored clothing, under the edges of carpets, and in air ducts, where they eat pet hair and other organic debris. A recent infestation in my home originated from a dead animal carcass within a wall void. These little beasts are also *serious* pests of insect collections, and every novice or serious collector has eventually had to deal with them.

The sight of adult dermestids around light fixtures and windows suggests a larval infestation somewhere in the house. Often, significant damage has been done before the insects are discovered. When an infestation is found, *immediately* check all closets for damaged woolen goods as well as any carpets made of animal materials.

CONTROL Prevention is far better than any cure, but there are effective insecticides if that fails.

- Woolens and other vulnerable fabrics should be dry-cleaned or laundered before storing. Clothing stored in closed containers should be packed with mothballs or paradichlorobenzene flakes. Mothballs and PDB are also effective in preventing infestations in insect collections. INSECTICIDES SHOULD NOT BE USED TO TREAT CLOTHING. The one exception is moth-proofing solution applied by professional dry cleaners.
- Vacuuming removes both beetles and larvae, along with hair and lint that could support future infestations.
- Insecticides may be applied to infested areas of the home. Materials of choice include chloropyrifos, permethrin, and bendiocarb. Elimination of widespread ongoing problems may require the assistance of a professional pest control operator.

Indian Meal Moths
You'll Need More than a Fly Swatter to Get Rid of Them!

I remember the day vividly. I had just written a column on Indian meal moths for the *Atlanta Journal-Constitution*. I opened the door to our walk-in pantry in search of some olive oil and was greeted by the very pests I had just described. A horde of tiny, delicate moths zigzagged upward on fragile wings like fluffy dust balls riding an updraft. The ones that didn't succumb to my clapping hands managed to grab a foothold high on the walls and ceiling. On closer inspection, I saw their small, yellowish larvae high in the closet, surrounded by silken webbing and ready to pupate. About once every 6 months, I find that my pantry has been invaded by Indian meal moths. The next step is always to identify the infested food products and get rid of them.

SCIENTIFIC NAMES Order Lepidoptera; Family Pyralidae; *Plodia interpunctella* (Hubner)

IDENTIFICATION The adult Indian meal moth is reddish brown, about ⅜ inch long, and has a wingspan of about ¾ inch. When at rest, the wings are folded back over the body. The caterpillars, which are about ⅔ inch long when fully grown, have black heads and a "dirty white" body that is sometimes tinged with pink or green. They produce unsightly webbing that sticks pieces of food together.

BIOLOGY Female moths lay between sixty and three hundred eggs singly or in groups on or near foodstuffs in cupboards and pantries. The eggs hatch in 2–14 days, and the tiny white larvae disperse within hours, invading a variety of foods. The development time varies, depending on temperature,

To stop an Indian meal moth infestation, you must find the source.

from 2 to 4 weeks. In a warm pantry, it is closer to 4 weeks. When they are ready to pupate, the larvae often migrate a considerable distance from the food source, sometimes moving into cracks or crevices, sometimes crawling to the top of the cupboard or up walls to where the wall and ceiling meet. Here they spin their cocoons and undergo metamorphosis, and a new generation of moths emerges to repeat the life cycle. Sometimes the first sign of an infestation is the appearance of adults flying around the home in the evening. They are attracted to lights and often appear in front of the television set.

IMPACT It is the larval, or caterpillar, stage that causes the damage. The larvae feed on a wide variety of food products, including flour and meal, dried fruits, dried pet foods, and bird food. The larvae spin a web as they feed, and leave behind trails of silk as they move through the food. Small particles of food often stick loosely to these threads, making the trail very visible.

CONTROL Prompt action and diligence are important in keeping this pest under control. The following steps will help.

- Before purchasing, examine foods for broken and damaged packages to avoid bringing stored pests into the home. Check package dates to ensure freshness. Do not allow stored food products and spices to go unused for long periods.
- YOU MUST FIND THE SOURCE OF THE INFESTATION! When infested packages are found in the pantry, discard them immediately. There is no satisfactory method of separating insects from food products.
- Place the contents of open uninfested packages in glass jars with tight-fitting tops. (There is a possibility that eggs were laid in these products and may hatch later, leading to a new infestation.)
- Remove all food containers from the infested area (shelf paper may also need to be removed) and clean it, concentrating on cracks and crevices. Remove and destroy all cocoons on ceilings.
- Questionable or very lightly infested containers can be frozen at 0 degrees for 4–7 days and then used.
- Continue to observe the area for several months after treatment. If moths reappear, the cleanup may have been inadequate, or newly infested packages may have been brought into the home.

Though pesticides are not usually recommended for use around foods, a few products can be used as an additional "clean-out" measure for serious infestations. These include pyrethrins, resmethrin in ready-to-use fogs, tetramethrin aerosol spray, and cyfluthrin aerosol fogger. When using any pesticide, *always* follow the instructions on the label.

Cigarette Beetles

More than Just a Tobacco Pest

When I was a graduate student at Virginia Tech, the antismoking movement was just coming into flower. In keeping with this crusade, one of the radio stations in Radford, Virginia, featured a woman called "Pack-a-day Polly" who pitched little segments twenty times a day that went something like this: "Pack-a-day Polly here. Time for your twelfth cigarette." The idea was that if smokers lit up *only* when Polly told them to, they would bring their habit down to a pack a day. One Monday morning a friend of mine came into the lab complaining loudly about Pack-a-day Polly. I asked why he was so angry. After all, she was getting the serious smokers to reduce their consumption. "That's the problem," he snarled. "I'd almost quit, and now she's gotten me back up to a pack a day." Although Pack-a-day Polly

Cigarette beetles are a major pantry pest.

may have had a positive effect on many western Virginia smokers, she had absolutely none on the cigarette beetle. It has yet to lower its tobacco consumption. A specimen of this native Egyptian species was found in King Tutankhamen's tomb! And in the 3,500 years since, this diminutive demon has changed very little.

SCIENTIFIC NAMES Order Coleoptera; Family Anobiidae; *Lasioderma serricorne* (Fabricius)

IDENTIFICATION This tiny insect, only ⅛ inch long, is one of the most common of our pantry pests. The cigarette beetle is oval when viewed from above, light to dark brown in color, with smooth outer wings. The head is bent down almost at a right angle to the body, giving the insect a humpbacked appearance in side view. The antennae are serrate (i.e., the edges of the segments are pointed, like the teeth of a saw). The larvae are cream colored and adorned with fine hairs.

BIOLOGY Cigarette beetles occur throughout the year but may be a bit more common in the fall and winter months. They are strong fliers and are attracted to lights. It is not unusual to find them around a lamp or TV screen. Adults live about 2–4 weeks. Females lay their eggs (about one hundred in their lifetime) directly on food that can be eaten by the larvae. The eggs are oval, white, and almost too small to be seen with the naked eye. Larvae are yellowish white and grublike, and when fully grown are about ⅛ inch long. The larva spins a cocoon before pupating. The total time from egg to adult averages about 6–8 weeks, and there are about three to six generations a year.

IMPACT Cigarette beetles infest a wide variety of food products, including cigarettes, cigars, chickpeas, cassava, paprika, peanuts, rhubarb, rice, cumin, dates, and many other spices and seeds. They also feed on dried insects, leather, furniture stuffing, and bookbinding paste.

CONTROL Like other pantry pests, the first step in controlling this insect is to find and eliminate the source of the infestation. Prevention and exclusion are the principal methods for ongoing control. Inspect all dried foods in the infested area, whether it is in a pantry, drawer, or cabinet. Once found, destroy the infested material. Clean out the cupboard/pantry/drawers thoroughly. A vacuum cleaner is excellent for this. After you are finished, throw away the bag. Next, seal up all susceptible foods in containers that will not allow adults or larvae to get to them.

Saw-toothed Grain Beetles
Big Problem in a Small Package

There's an old wives' tale (OK, to be fair, we can also refer to it as an ancient husbands' anecdote) about things occurring in "threes." And so it has proven to be with pantry pests. After my columns on Indian meal moths and cigarette beetles, I received several notes from readers who had been dealing with those pests as well as several queries about another frequent pantry invader—the saw-toothed grain beetle. Those questions brought back some fond memories (and a few nightmares) of my life as a graduate student. The saw-toothed grain beetle was the first pantry infestation I remember having to deal with as a young graduate student living on my own. This tiny creature can be a worthy adversary when it comes to protecting the stored products in your cupboard.

SCIENTIFIC NAMES Order Coleoptera; Family Silvanidae; *Oryzaephilus surinamensis* (Linnaeus)

IDENTIFICATION Saw-toothed grain beetles are dark brown, *very* flattened, slender, about 1/10 inch long, with the abdomen tapering toward the tip. Viewed under a strong hand lens or microscope, the beetle has six sharp, toothlike projections along each side of the thorax—hence the name. (If the insect were of the appropriate length, you probably could grab it by the rear end and do a decent job cutting firewood with those teeth!) The larvae are elongate, yellowish white, and about 1/8 inch long when ready to pupate.

BIOLOGY These insects readily penetrate packaged material—including but not limited to cereals, candies, dried fruits, flour, meal, tobacco, macaroni, nuts, chocolate, sugar, drugs, and dried meats. Females lay between 45 and

Adult beetles live up to 3 years.

285 shiny white eggs in the food material they infest, either singly or in clusters. The life cycle takes 30–50 days depending on temperature, and there can be as many as seven generations a year. The mature larvae usually make a pupal case out of pieces of food particles held together with a sticky oral secretion. Adults typically live 6–10 months but have been known to live more than 3 years.

IMPACT Its flat body allows the saw-toothed grain beetle to penetrate even the smallest openings to get into stored food materials. In addition to contaminating foodstuffs, the beetles may also wander away from the infested material and can be found elsewhere inside cupboards, the pantry, or other rooms of the house.

CONTROL As with other pantry pests, any control *must* begin with the location and elimination of infested food items. Every potential food source should be checked, and if infested should be discarded. The beetles are often found in *unopened* boxes of food material. Some items may be salvaged by freezing for a week. Empty and thoroughly vacuum the cupboards, paying special attention to cracks and crevices. As a precaution against reinfestation, store susceptible foods in sealed containers or in the refrigerator or freezer until you are certain the beetles have been eliminated.

If a pesticide is to be used, cyfluthrin or pyrethrins plus piperonyl butoxide are good choices. Contact your local county extension agent for the most recent recommendations. When using a pesticide, especially in the kitchen, *always* follow the directions on the label.

Clothes Moths

They Can Turn Your Riches to Rags

Ah, the joys of Christmas. Early morning adventures under the tree; the exchange of presents with loved ones; your one-year-old enjoying the box more than the toy that came in it; the inescapable afternoon nap after that tryptophan-laden turkey dinner; your daughter trying on the new cashmere sweater from her sweetheart (she doesn't dare tell him that clothes moths ate holes in the one he gave her last year). Insect pests pop up in the oddest

Clothes moths can make a mess of cashmere sweaters.

places, and when you least expect them. If Ray Stevens had been singing about them instead of Santa Claus in his popular Christmas song, he'd have made only a minor pronoun change: "They're EVERYWHERE, they're EVERYWHERE!"

SCIENTIFIC NAMES Order Lepidoptera; Family Tineidae; Case-making clothes moth: *Tinea pellionella*; Webbing clothes moth: *Tineola bisselliella*

IDENTIFICATION Two species are common in the Atlanta area: the case-making clothes moth and the webbing clothes moth. Both are buff colored and have wingspans of about ½ inch. The larvae are small, cream colored with dark head capsules, and are about ½ inch long when they are ready to pupate.

BIOLOGY Clothes moths are not commonly seen because they avoid lights. Adults prefer dark, undisturbed places like attics, basements, and closets. They often sequester themselves in dark corners or in the folds of fabric. Though the adults do not feed, they lay dozens of eggs that hatch into tiny, voracious fabric-eating machines. Larvae of case-making moths spin a silken case around themselves and drag their ever-enlarging home with them wherever they go. Webbing moth larvae spin silken tunnels that combine cloth fragments and bits of fecal material.

IMPACT Clothes moth larvae feed on a wide variety of organic material, including wool, hair, leather, feathers, paper, silk, linen, cotton, and even some synthetic fibers. They especially like fabric that has been soiled with urine, beverages, or sweat. Damage may consist of surface feeding or complete holes eaten through the garment. Frequently used clothing is much less likely to be damaged than clothing stored for long periods. Items commonly attacked include carpets, blankets, wool sweaters, down pillows, stuffed animals, and upholstered furniture. Larvae may even live in air ducts, feeding on lint, pet hair, and other debris.

CONTROL Proper cleaning and storage of fabrics are essential for control and prevention. The following measures will help to keep clothes moths at bay.

- Locate the source of the problem prior to any treatment. Inspect closets and stored clothing for damage, moths, and larvae. Look along carpet edges, along baseboards, in stored clothing, and in the furs and feathers of stuffed animals.
- Any infested clothing should be discarded or cleaned and treated professionally. It is best *not* to treat clothing with insecticides. Rugs and wall voids may be sprayed with pyrethrins.
- Never leave clothing, rugs, or any other fabrics in untended piles for long periods.
- Use a vacuum cleaner with a crevice tool to remove debris from baseboards, upholstered furniture, and other places where the moths may accumulate.
- Because egg-laying moths are attracted to soiled articles, clean them quickly. Ironing will destroy all stages of these pests.
- Constant light in closets will discourage moths, and freezing has been used successfully for moth control.
- Fabrics can be placed in polyethylene bags. Remove all the air to minimize condensation, then freeze for at least 3 days.

To avoid accidental poisoning by naphthalene and paradichlorobenzene (PDB), use extreme care when using mothballs or moth flakes containing these materials.

Fleas

If Thou Hast an Indoor Pet, Thou Shalt Have Them

There is an old axiom among pest control specialists that when Moses came down from the mountain, he was carrying an extra stone tablet. But he tripped on the way down and the tablet fell to the ground and shattered. This was very unfortunate because this tablet contained an eleventh commandment which read: "If thou hast an indoor pet, thou shalt have fleas." Even people who don't have pets can be invaded. Case in point: When I lived in Griffin years ago, we had no indoor pets. But my in-laws from Virginia came to visit us and brought along their two chihuahuas. For the duration of their visit, no fleas were seen. But two weeks after they left, we were invaded by small, hungry, uninvited houseguests in search of a blood meal. Because there were no pets on which they could feast, they sought out any warm bodies they could find—in this case ME AND MY FAMILY! That happened only once; thereafter, I was prepared with an adequate control program that I implemented *immediately* after my in-laws left.

Fleas will always have a special place in human history because one species, the Oriental rat flea, was the vector of the bubonic plague, the Black Death that ravaged Europe in the mid-1300s. This disease, caused by the bacillus *Yersinia pestis*, was so infectious and so deadly that not enough people were left in some cities to bury the dead. The bacillus surfaced on the West Coast of the United States in 1904, and a residual population still exists in some western rodent species. And, yes, some native fleas in that area are capable of transmitting the disease. The disease is not known in the Southeast.

SCIENTIFIC NAMES Order Siphonaptera; Family Pulicidae; Cat flea: *Ctenocephalides felis* (Bouche); Dog flea: *Ctenocephalides canis* (Curtis)

Fleas have back legs made for jumping.

IDENTIFICATION Adult fleas are small, brown to brownish black insects about 1/16 inch long. They are flattened side to side so they can move easily among the hairs of their hosts.

BIOLOGY Fleas spend almost all of their lives on our pets. They mate there, and after every blood meal each female lays up to fifty eggs a day (four hundred in a lifetime). The tiny, whitish, oval eggs fall to the ground soon after they are laid and hatch in 1–10 days into slender, white, wormlike larvae. These tiny worms thrive down in the nap of carpets, beneath furniture cushions, and along the baseboards, where they are virtually invisible. They feed on organic matter that may consist of both animal and plant debris, including dried blood and adult flea feces. Mature larvae spin camouflaged silken cocoons that are difficult to see because they incorporate pieces of debris found in their habitat. These cocoons help to protect the developing fleas from pesticides. The pupal stage lasts from a week to several months, depending on temperature. Adults emerge from these cocoons after a physical disturbance *or* when warm-blooded animals are present (and we humans *are* warm-blooded animals!).

IMPACT Fleas cause discomfort and irritation to both pets and people. It has been estimated that flea bites account for more than half of all dermatological conditions requiring veterinary assistance. A single flea bite on a hypersensitive person or pet can cause intense itching and irritation. Unlike some other insects, both sexes bite. Newly emerged adult fleas are ravenous for a blood meal. This is why vacationers are often inundated with fleas on their return home *or* a non–pet owner is overrun with fleas about 2 weeks after a pet-packing guest has departed.

The cat flea (which infests *both* dogs and cats) is an intermediate host for the dog tapeworm. Dogs, cats, and sometimes people are infected with the tapeworm when the infected flea is accidentally swallowed. One study estimated that 24 percent of all dogs and 30 percent of all cats carry this tapeworm. Another study showed that a little over 1 percent of all fleas are infected with the tapeworm.

CONTROL Good flea control includes several steps.

- **Treat your pets** Several solid programs are available. Consult your vet for recommendations that best suit your pet's needs. These may include a special comb designed to remove adult fleas from your pet's hair. Insecticidal shampoos provide short-term control, and spot applications using fipronil or oral pills that include cythioate are new products offering long-term satisfaction.

- **Vacuum** Before any insecticides are applied indoors, a thorough vacuuming is necessary to pick up many of the adult fleas present in your carpets, furniture, or other places your pet may frequent. A heavy-duty vacuum cleaner is recommended, and you may wish to have the carpets professionally cleaned. After vacuuming, take the vacuum cleaner outside and discard the bag.

- **Indoor treatment** Spot-treat areas pets frequent the most—both on the floor and on furniture, especially beneath cushions. Use a product that contains both an adulticide (something that will kill the adult fleas) *and* methoprine (sometimes called Precor). The latter material is very effective for long-term control of larvae. It can be purchased at your local hardware or grocery store. Be sure that both materials are on the label. Do not touch treated areas until the pesticides are completely dry.

- **Outdoor treatment** Outside treatment is essential, especially if your pet moves freely back and forth from outside to inside. Treat the areas your pet frequents the most. In spots where there is excessive debris or litter, increase the volume of water in the spray to get more complete coverage. Remember that when using pesticides, you should *always* follow the directions on the label.

Head Lice

The Cooties Are Coming!

This chapter is going to be lousy—and nitpicking. Yes, I'm going to talk about . . . head lice. Sometimes called "cooties," these little pests often seem to pop up out of nowhere. They seem to be more common just as kids go back to school. At one time children who had head lice were stigmatized because lice were erroneously associated with dirt and the lower socioeconomic stratum. In truth, these pests show no preference for any particular income level, nor should they suggest a lack of hygiene or sanitation. In fact, they may actually prefer freshly washed hair, because the nits can stick more easily to clean hair than to oily hair. I am happy to say that this stigma has now been largely dismissed.

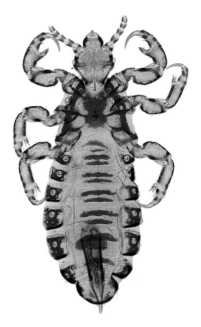

Head lice use claws to hold on to hair.

SCIENTIFIC NAMES Order Phthiraptera; Family Pediculidae; *Pediculus humanus capitis* De Geer

IDENTIFICATION Head lice are reddish brown, wingless insects about 1/16 to 1/8 inch long. They may be difficult to detect because symptoms like itching and scratching are not always apparent. The oval, grayish white eggs, called nits, are cemented to the hair shaft, often very close to the scalp on the nape of the neck or behind the ears. A nit can be distinguished from dirt simply by trying to slide it up the hair shaft using your fingers. Eggs are usually difficult to move, while other pieces of debris in the hair slide easily. Head lice move from one host to another by direct contact and on shared combs, brushes, hats, and other hair accessories. Though they can remain on bedding, carpeting, and furniture for brief periods, lice usually cannot survive without a host for more than 24 hours.

BIOLOGY The eggs hatch in 5–10 days and the light-colored nymphs immediately begin to feed. Development time from egg to adult is about 18–20 days, and adults live for about 1 month.

LOUSE DETECTION

If itching/scratching is not present but you know that children who associate with yours are infested, try this conditioner/comb technique:

- Apply conditioner to dry hair, trying to cover all the hairs from root to tip.
- Detangle hair, using an ordinary comb.
- Comb through hair with a fine-tooth comb.
- Wipe conditioner off the comb onto a paper tissue and look for lice and eggs.
- Repeat combing for each part of the head at least five times.
- Also examine the comb for eggs and lice.
- If you find lice, your child should be treated.

IMPACT The most notable effect of head lice is the personal embarrassment that accompanies their discovery. Though these insects have little medical impact, their presence often generates considerable alarm from both parents and school officials. Their feeding can cause intense itching, and if left untreated can result in skin and scalp irritations and loss of sleep. Children, particularly those in elementary school, are more likely to get head lice because of their close interactions with one another (sharing combs, hats, brushes, etc.). Individuals infested at school may infest other family members at home.

CONTROL The best way to avoid head lice is to avoid head-to-head contact with other people, including the sharing of combs, brushes, and hats. A child who has exhibited the symptoms for head lice should be examined by someone who knows how to identify the insects *and* their eggs. A novice might mistake nits and lice for dandruff, globs of hair oil, or dried flakes of hairspray. The average number of lice per person is low: only about five to ten. Therefore, careful inspection, particularly along the back of the neck and around the ears, is especially important. Once an infestation has been determined, a shampoo containing a chemical control agent can be used. These are available at your pharmacy without prescription. After 7 days, the hair should again be inspected, and if lice or eggs are still present, a second application will be needed.

Termites

Your Home Is Their Sunday Buffet

Spring is here. The dogwoods are blooming in Piedmont Park, the azaleas are in flower at Augusta, the Georgia Renaissance Festival is gearing up for another season, and deep inside the bowels of your woodwork, termites may be literally eating you out of house and home. Perhaps no single insect pest generates more angst or has more economic impact for homeowners than termites.

Each spring, cloying swarms of small black insects appear in and around our homes. From February to October, underground termite colonies produce reproductive forms—males and females—that spew out in a roiling swarm of termite sex. Each mated pair begins a new colony, and they may live together in conjugal bliss for as long as 20 years.

SCIENTIFIC NAMES Order Isoptera; Family Rhinotermitidae; Eastern subterranean termite: *Reticulitermes flavipes* (Kollar); Formosan subterranean termite: *Coptotermes formosanus* (Shiraki); Family Kalotermitidae; West Indian powderpost termite: *Cryptotermes brevis* (Walker)

IDENTIFICATION Termite workers are wingless, creamy white, and about ¼ to ⅜ inch long. They are the most common form within the colony and the one that homeowners will find feeding on the wood of our homes. The adults emerge in spring and early summer, and to the untrained eye closely resemble flying ants. Termites, however, have a "boxy" body; that is, no constriction separates the thorax (where the legs are) from the abdomen. Ants have a distinct and narrow waist, like Hollywood's version of a beautiful woman. Termites have straight, filamentous antennae, like a tiny string of pearls; ants have bent, or elbowed, antennae. All four wings of termites are about equal in size; ants have much larger front wings.

BIOLOGY Subterranean termites are social insects that live in colonies consisting of fifty thousand to five hundred thousand individuals, depending on the species and time of year. Each colony has several castes in addition to the winged reproductives, including one or more worker forms that resemble small, white grubs with legs. They are the ones responsible for the damage. In their natural state, termites are very important recyclers of dead wood on the forest floor. They feed on dead limbs and stumps and enrich the soil. But when they feed on our home, they can become a nightmare. These little devils enter houses through cracks as tiny as 1/64 inch, traveling through small mud tubes that wind their way upward along the walls

Termites can literally eat you out of house and home.

of the foundation. These mud galleries are often hard to see because they work their way inside the foundation, through cracks in the cinder blocks or concrete, and eventually into the wood structure itself—which is, of course, their dinner table.

IMPACT Every year, termites cause upward of $2.5 billion in damage in the United States; Atlanta ranks number five in the country for termite damage.

CONTROL Homeowners spend millions of dollars each year treating their homes to prevent termites and repairing damage already done. An adequate inspection and control program is a must for every homeowner in the South.

Detection Though the termite swarm is often the first sign that termites have established a tooth-hold in your home, annual inspections by pest control operators are important in order to find infestations before they become severe. If you have an adequate crawlspace beneath your home, you can do a cursory examination yourself. The telltale mud tubes are very distinctive. If you find one, call your pest control operator immediately. The problem with the do-it-yourself approach is that the average homeowner is not adequately prepared to make a detailed inspection. Most pest control companies offer free inspections and will generally do a much more thorough job.

What Should You Do If Termites Are Found? This is not a job you want to do yourself. Get estimates from several pest control operators. Estimates are usually free, and you will get an inspection, a chart showing problem areas in your home, and a treatment plan. Do not necessarily take the lowest bid. *Know* what the company is offering and what it will guarantee. As protection for your investment, it is a good idea to purchase a termite bond to guard against future damage. There are two basic types: (1) a treatment bond in

TERMITES OR ANTS?

At the same time that termites are swarming, several species of ants are also producing mating swarms. The ants are, in general, rather harmless and present no major threat other than being a nuisance to homeowners. So, how do we tell the difference? There are several easy-to-see clues. Termites have rather straight antennae that resemble a thin string of pearls. Ants have an "elbow" in their antennae, which bend at almost a 90-degree angle. Termites have a broad connection between the thorax (where the legs are) and the abdomen. Ants, which are related to wasps, have a distinct "waist." Finally, the front and rear pairs of wings are almost equal in length in termites, while ants have much larger front wings.

which the company will re-treat your home for free, but you are responsible for any damages; (2) a repair bond in which the company is responsible for the repairs. The best plan, of course, covers termite damage.

The pest control industry has many honest, reputable firms, but there are less than trustworthy ones out there as well. If you feel that the service you received was not acceptable, the state Department of Agriculture will send an inspector to see if your treatment was applied according to standard. The inspector will take soil samples to determine the quality and quantity of the pesticide used. This test can be done any time within 6 months of the termiticide application.

Treatment: Chemicals or Baits? A few years ago, a single application of a persistent pesticide might have given 25–30 years of protection if the barrier was left undisturbed. But those chemicals are no longer available to us. Today, the homeowner must choose between several alternatives, each of which must be viewed as temporary and part of an ongoing process. Bait systems are typically used to reduce the number of termites in a colony so that it is no longer a threat to the house. Pesticides offer a barrier to prevent these pests from entering. A good treatment plan may include either or both, depending on your specific needs.

Tips for the Homeowner

- Have an annual inspection, preferably by a company with whom you now have a termite bond.
- Keep moisture away from your foundation. Be sure gutters, downspouts, and air-conditioning condensation drains are working properly and drain away from the house.
- Keep mulch at least 2 feet from the foundation. Gravel is preferred to bark or sawdust.
- Remove any wood debris from beneath your house and from around the foundation.
- Open vents to crawl spaces during warmer weather to reduce moisture.
- If chemicals have been used for termite control, do not disturb or disrupt the termiticide-treated soil barrier near the foundation.
- For new home construction, discuss termites with your builder *prior* to construction to avoid building practices that encourage termite entry.

Camel Crickets

Humpbacked Moisture Lovers

What are those strange-looking, long-legged, humpbacked creatures that have moved into the basement and crawl space? They are camel crickets (sometimes called cave crickets). Unlike their melodious field cricket cousins, these insects do not sing or chirp.

SCIENTIFIC NAMES Order Orthoptera; Family Gryllacrididae; *Ceuthophilus* spp.

The camel cricket's strong back legs allow it to leap great distances.

IDENTIFICATION As the name implies, the camel cricket has an unusual humpbacked appearance; the head seems to be tucked down between the front legs. The antennae are much longer than the body, and though these crickets are wingless, the long, drumstick-shaped femurs of the hind legs help them leap prodigious distances.

BIOLOGY Most camel crickets are nocturnal and are found in areas of high humidity and moisture. Outside, they are found under logs, stones, in piles of firewood, in overgrown vegetation, in damp leaves, and — yes — in caves. Within these harborages, camel crickets pass the winter as adults or immatures. In early spring the adult females begin laying eggs in the soil, and within a few weeks the nymphs hatch. Nymphs look almost exactly like adults except for their smaller size and, in females, lack of an ovipositor (the egg-laying device at the rear of the body). Camel crickets feed on a wide variety of organic matter, including fungus and mold, and outside they can cause damage to plants and lawn furniture made of fabric.

IMPACT Camel crickets can become a problem for homeowners when they move indoors, which often occurs following extremes in weather conditions like extended dry periods or excessive rainfall. As with their outdoor habitats, they are attracted inside to cool, moist areas such as basements, storage buildings, crawl spaces, and garages. I once found about two dozen of them in a sink in the bathroom at one of our state parks! Camel crickets are mostly a nuisance problem, but they can damage indoor plants and fabrics, including rugs, furniture, draperies, books, canvas, boxes, linen, and other articles of clothing, especially if they are stored in boxes that remain damp.

CONTROL Because moisture is a primary requirement for camel crickets, removing moist habitats is paramount for effective, long-lasting control. Preventing access to your home is very important as well.

- Remove tall weeds and grass near the home.
- Seal small openings with caulk or screening, including access to dryer vents and crawl spaces.
- Ventilate crawl spaces, basements, and outbuildings to reduce moisture.
- In storage areas, stack boxes on pallets away from the wall.
- Do not make woodpiles near entrances to your home.
- Keep leaf mulch and wood/bark chips at least a foot from the foundation.
- Use sticky boards in corners and behind appliances to catch crickets that have already come inside.

If camel crickets remain a problem after the above remedies have been followed, chemical control may be necessary. Focus applications around the border of the structure, especially at possible entrance points (doors, windows, vents, etc.). Spray only when the population is very large or when valuable materials are threatened. Contact your local county extension office for the most recent recommendations.

Earwigs

Horror Movie Monsters

Folklore says that earwigs enter the ears of sleepers and bore into the brain. Sounds like another B-grade horror flick, doesn't it? Of course, there is no truth to this repulsive tale. Someone recently wrote to tell me that earwigs had invaded her new home in large numbers. If the folktales about them *were* true, I would have had to recommend immediate evacuation of the premises and a call to every pest control operator within a hundred miles, and maybe the army, too.

SCIENTIFIC NAMES Order Dermaptera; Family Forficulidae

IDENTIFICATION Earwigs have a macabre appearance that perfectly comple-ments their folklore reputation. They are elongate, flattened insects, varying in color according to species from black to reddish brown. But their most distinctive characteristic is a pair of forceps-like appendages (sometimes called pinchers) on the end of the abdomen. Females have smaller, straight-sided forceps (technically called cerci); those of males are much larger, un-equal in size, and curved. Earwigs may be winged or wingless; when wings

Rear "pinchers" distinguish the earwig.

are present, the first pair are hard, short, and beetle-like. The second pair are membranous, fan shaped, and fold up beneath the hard front pair. The two most common species are about ½ to ⅗ inch long when mature.

Earwigs can occur in large numbers, especially in hot, dry weather.

BIOLOGY Earwigs develop through gradual metamorphosis, with the immature stages greatly resembling the adults. In spring or fall, the female lays a brood of eggs in an underground chamber in the upper 2–3 inches of soil. She stays with her clutch of eggs, tending them until they hatch. The young then take care of themselves for the year or so that it takes them to mature. Both immatures and adults overwinter in the soil, sometimes digging as far down as *6 feet* to escape freezing temperatures! They rarely fly and are unable to crawl very long distances, so they hitchhike instead, catching free rides on cut flowers, newspapers, cardboard boxes, baskets of fruit and vegetables, and so on. They need cool, moist places, and basements and damp crawl spaces, compost piles, and woodpiles are perfect places for them to hide during the day. They come out at night and scavenge on decaying animal and plant material. They are also attracted to lights.

IMPACT Earwigs sometimes occur in large numbers indoors, particularly in hot, dry weather. Homeowners will find them along the foundations of the home and in crawl spaces where it is cool and damp. They are also common in mulched flower beds. They will enter buildings through any available cracks and crevices. Though earwigs do not bite, they will attempt to pinch with their cerci if handled. With larger specimens this can be a bit painful.

CONTROL The old adage "an ounce of prevention is worth a pound of cure" is applicable for earwigs. Though they are easily killed by residual pesticides placed beneath cabinets, in cracks and crevices, along baseboards, and so on, the resulting control will be of relatively short duration because more will enter from outside.

The *first* step in earwig control should be to eliminate their entryways.

- Use caulking compound, putty, and weather stripping around windows, doors, pipes, and other entry points.
- Reduce moisture in crawl spaces and around the house foundation by making sure gutters carry water *away* from the foundation.
- Make a dry border adjacent to the house using stone or gravel instead of organic mulch.

Silverfish and Firebrats

No Laughing Matter

The names silverfish and firebrat may conjure up images of some old-fashioned comedy team akin to Laurel and Hardy, but these little pests can become a nuisance to the homeowner if populations get out of hand.

SCIENTIFIC NAMES Order Thysanura; Family Lepismatidae; *Lepisma saccharina* Linnaeus; *Ctenolepisma* sp.; *Thermobia domestica* (Packard)

IDENTIFICATION Silverfish are flat, wingless, often silver to gray insects. Their color comes from tiny silver scales that give the body a metallic sheen. The body is ½ to ¾ inch long and tapers carrotlike from head to tail. Two long antennae extend from the head and usually wrap around the body, and from the tail three long, slender "bristles" extend to the rear. Firebrats resemble silverfish but lack the silvery sheen. They are brown to gray with dark spots that give them a mottled appearance.

Silverfish prefer warm, moist locations.

BIOLOGY The time needed for a silverfish to develop from egg to adult varies from 3 months to 3 years. Firebrats usually take about 4 months. Adults may live for up to 3 years and will molt throughout their lives, sometimes more than thirty times a year. Depending on the species, the adult female lays clutches of five to fifty eggs in cracks and crevices near food sources. The nymphs look like the adults except for being smaller and white. Both silverfish and firebrats are most active at night and move swiftly, often stopping briefly before scurrying on. They move with a wriggling motion reminiscent of swimming fish. Because their populations increase very slowly, large numbers indicate a longtime infestation.

IMPACT Silverfish can be found almost anywhere in the house, but they favor moist, warm locations—especially around sinks and other plumbing—and undisturbed storage areas where the humidity is high. They are frequently found *in* sinks or bathtubs because they fall in while seeking moisture and cannot climb out. Homeowners often see them when they move storage boxes or open a cabinet door. Firebrats prefer areas of high temperature (90 degrees and above) and high humidity. They are more common in attics and around ovens, furnaces, water heaters, and hot water pipes. Both silverfish and firebrats often enter homes in paper, books, food, starched clothing, and furniture.

These insects are primarily considered nuisance pests. They do feed on a wide variety of materials, including book bindings, starch in clothing, linen, dried organic ornaments, wallpaper, paste, and glue, but damage is significant only with large infestations over long periods.

CONTROL Good sanitation is a major step in controlling silverfish and firebrats. When storing items, especially fabrics, be sure they are clean and starch free. Keep everything in tight-fitting containers and reduce moisture as much as possible. Because these pests often reside in wall cavities, keep storage boxes a few inches away from walls and off the floor.

If sanitation alone is not sufficient, various pesticides will eliminate silverfish and firebrats or at least reduce their numbers. Available sprays for ants and roaches in pump sprayers or aerosol cans are usually effective. These include acephate, cypermethrin, diazinon, Baygon, and pyrethrins. Boric acid can be puffed into cracks and crevices and applied loosely around the storage area. It has the advantage of being very low in toxicity and very long lasting if applied in dry voids where it will remain undisturbed.

Control may not be necessary if populations are low and limited to small areas, and no damage is noticed.

Household Insects

RELATIVES

Daddy-longlegs

Alien Invaders?

At first glance it looks like something out of *War of the Worlds*. Moving slowly and clumsily over the ground with its compact body suspended over long, stilted legs, this creature might be going to an audition for the next *Star Wars* movie. But, no, it's just a daddy-longlegs looking for its next meal.

SCIENTIFIC NAMES Order Opiliones; Family Phalangidae

IDENTIFICATION One of the myths surrounding these creatures is that they are the most poisonous spiders on Earth. But they are neither spiders nor poisonous — at least not to humans. Daddy-longlegs, sometimes called harvestmen, are often mistaken for spiders, but they are more closely related to ticks and mites. They have eight *very* long, very slender legs. These legs sometimes reach a length of 2 or 3 inches and support a relatively small, boxlike body that is usually dark brown or gray.

BIOLOGY Adult females lay their eggs in the fall, either on the ground or in rotten wood such as dead stumps or logs. They are usually found in areas of relatively high humidity or where moisture is abundant, and often drink from tiny puddles and other sources of water. The eggs hatch in spring, and the tiny white immatures that emerge (their color darkens within a few days) are carbon copies of their adult counterparts. These arachnids will undergo seven molts on the way to adulthood, which they will reach later in the year. Daddy-longlegs do not have fangs. They capture prey with their pincher-like chelicerae, which they then use to tear their food into smaller, more manageable pieces.

Though they appear slow and lethargic, harvestmen can move quickly

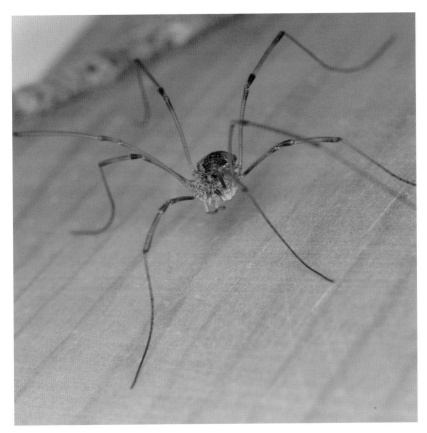

Daddy-longlegs are harmless to humans.

when disturbed. They are usually nocturnal, and are sometimes found in bunches in protected sites, their legs all intertwined. One of their more interesting protective mechanisms is their ability to "shed" a leg if necessary to make good an escape. The leg falls away and lies twitching on the ground while the daddy-longlegs scurries away to safety. Lost legs are not regenerated.

IMPACT There are many species of harvestmen, and most prey on smaller insects, spiders, and other arthropods. They also commonly feed on dead organisms. A few species feed on organic debris or the juices of selected plants.

CONTROL Though they are rarely found indoors, daddy-longlegs do occasionally come inside in fairly large numbers. Then they become a nuisance. The best way to deal with them is to keep them from getting inside in the first place. Chemical barrier treatments or spot treatments may give temporary relief, but cleaning up trash or debris near the home, including stone piles and woodpiles, is a much better approach. Keep plants near the house trimmed back, and be sure to seal cracks and crevices around windows and doors. Also keep dampness down in basements by using dehumidifiers, and do not leave stacks of wet or damp towels or other fabrics around the house where harvestmen might be found.

Dust Mites
Gesundheit!

Cough, hack, gag, wheeze, sneeze, itch, and rub your watery eyes; 38 percent of Americans have some sort of allergy. And one of the biggest causes of allergies worldwide is the house dust mite. Some estimates credit this tiny beast with causing 25 percent of *all* human allergies.

SCIENTIFIC NAMES Order Acari; Family Pyroglyphidae; *Dermatophagoides* sp.

IDENTIFICATION House dust mites are microscopic creatures; they average about ¹⁄₁₀₀ inch in size, and their translucent bodies are not visible to the naked eye. To make a reasonable identification, at least a 10x hand lens is required. Several dust mites could fit on the dot at the end of this sentence. The adult house mite's body has simple striations on both the top and the bottom. The bottom, or ventrum, has long hairs that extend away from the edges of the body; smaller hairs cover the rest of its surface. Adults have eight legs (like spiders and scorpions), no eyes, no antennae, and a tough shell that, seen through a microscope, has a hard, spiny, almost fearsome appearance.

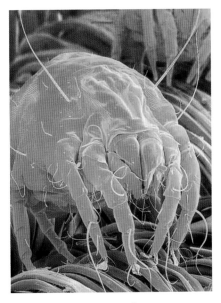

Dust mites contribute to allergies.

BIOLOGY Dust mites live on tiny dust particles that can be found in even the cleanest homes. The mites hide deep down in carpets, curtains, mattress seams, pillows, and other hard-to-clean spots where even the most obsessive housekeeper would never find them. The adult female lays forty to eighty eggs, either singly or in groups of three to five. The larvae that emerge have six legs, and an eight-legged nymph emerges from the first molt. The life cycle typically takes about 1 month, and the adult lives another 1–3 months after that. Though the diet is varied, the primary food is dander—skin scales—from animals, including humans. Because humans slough off a large quantity of skin scales daily, there is usually an abundant food supply available in every home. Seasonal temperature and humidity fluctuations have a major effect on mite populations. Because their bodies are 80 percent water, they prefer high humidity.

IMPACT Dust mites and their fecal discharge are the most common single allergen inhaled by people in the home. It has been estimated that 85 percent of asthmatics are allergic to this mite and its fecal material. When disturbed by standard vacuuming, the mites and their fecal pellets may remain airborne for up to 10 minutes. Common symptoms include sneezing, itching, wheezing, and watery eyes. The wheeze-inducing proteins are from digestive juices produced in the mite's gut.

CONTROL Although it is a never-ending battle, good sanitation practices will help to reduce numbers.

- Dust mites prefer wool and cotton to artificial fibers, so synthetic bedding materials are a better choice where mite problems have been determined. Special mite-resistant covers for pillows and mattresses are available.

- Sunlight destroys this pest. In the summer, put blankets and mattresses out in the sun, and dry your pillowcases and sheets on an outside clothesline.
- Daily vacuuming will reduce the amount of dust available to the mite. If possible, use vinyl flooring rather than carpeting because it harbors less dust.
- Dehumidifiers can reduce numbers because the mites prefer a moist environment.

Common House Spiders

Messy but Harmless

We walk into their webs in the dark. We curse them and kill them, then watch helplessly as they return in equal or greater numbers. Were it not for their persistent and unsightly webs they would be almost inconspicuous. But don't feel alone in your frustration. If the old expression "misery loves company" is applicable here, then you have a *lot* of sympathetic grumblers for company.

SCIENTIFIC NAMES Order Araneae; Family Theridiidae; *Achaearanea tepidariorum* (C. L. Koch)

IDENTIFICATION The common house spider, sometimes called the American house spider, is found worldwide. Although it belongs to the same family as the fabled black widow, it is totally harmless to humans. This spider is also smaller than the black widow, about ³⁄₁₆ to ⁵⁄₁₆ inch long (males are slightly smaller), and yellowish to brown in color, sometimes with a dusting of black speckles. The long legs are lighter yellow-brown with distinct annulations, or rings.

BIOLOGY The American house spider has adapted well to human environments and is rarely found in natural communities. It is quite at home in and around houses, sheds, and barns, and in many altered environments outdoors such as gardens, vacant lots, and cemeteries. Outside homes, house spiders are commonly found around lights, which attract insects that fly into their webs. But they are also major mess makers indoors, spinning their silken retreats wherever two surfaces come together—at junctures of roof and walls, at seams where two walls meet, in light fixtures, under

Common house spiders are frequent residents of our eaves and garages.

cabinets and furniture, and so on. The spider hangs in the center of her web, which to the untrained eye appears to be an irregular mass of silk, and waits for an insect to fly into the snare. If the web does not soon produce a suitable catch, the spider will move on and make a new one somewhere else, leaving the old web to collect dust and debris. This dainty creature can subdue prey as much as thirty times her size and eats even large beetles and cockroaches. Egg sacs containing one hundred to six hundred eggs are produced in late spring to late summer and hang freely in the web. Each sac is about ¼ inch in diameter and has a rugged papery cover. Adults live about 1 year, and each female may produce several egg cases. The first young spiderlings that hatch feed on undeveloped eggs before leaving the sac. They disperse by means of "ballooning," releasing tiny threads of silk that are caught up by air currents and carry them to new habitats.

IMPACT The common house spider, like most spiders, is a very beneficial creature. It feeds on a wide variety of insects, including a number of insect pests, but its webs do create an unsightly mess around the house.

CONTROL Elimination of most spiders should be avoided, if possible, because they aid in nuisance insect control. However, some things can be done to reduce their numbers around the home.

- Changing lights to yellow bulbs may help to reduce their attractiveness to insects, and thus to spiders.
- Keep outside areas free of excess vegetation and debris.
- Vacuum and dust both inside and outside, removing spiders, their egg sacs, and their webs.

Chemical control, if necessary, can be effective but must be repeated at regular intervals, depending on the directions on the product label. Materials effective for spiders can be purchased at local hardware or grocery stores. When using pesticides, *always* follow the instructions on the label.

Black Widows and Brown Recluses

Are They Really Husband Killers and Loners?

Throughout recorded history humans have shunned and feared spiders, generally regarding them as creepy, loathsome, and venomous creatures. Science fiction and superstition associate them with the eerie, deadly, and macabre. How unfair. Most spiders are very beneficial because they feed on insects, mites, and other small organisms humans find annoying.

The adult black widow is usually marked by a red hourglass beneath.

Almost all spiders possess venom glands that empty their contents through fangs at the end of the chelicerae, or "jaws." The venom is very poisonous to the small creatures that serve as the spiders' food, but in most cases is relatively harmless to humans. There are exceptions, of course. In Georgia, two small spider groups are of medical importance: the widow spiders and the brown recluse and its kin.

SCIENTIFIC NAMES Order Araneae; Family Theridiidae; Black widows: *Latrodectus* sp.; Family Loxoscelidae; Brown recluse: *Loxosceles reclusa* Gertsch and Mulaik

IDENTIFICATION Two species of black widow spiders are known in Georgia—the northern black widow and the southern black widow. Only the females of each species are poisonous to humans. The southern form is glossy black with long legs and a distinct red hourglass marking the bottom, or venter, of the abdomen; there is usually also a red spot just in front of the spinerettes, or silk glands, at the rear of the body. Mature adult females with

legs extended reach a length of 1½ inches. The harmless males are much smaller and typically have white or yellow and red lateral bands as well as a row of middorsal spots on the abdomen. Immature females may resemble the males. The northern form is *very* similar to the southern, but the hourglass on the venter is divided into two triangular spots that do not meet.

The brown recluse has a fiddle-shaped mark.

TREATMENT FOR SPIDER BITES

Because black widow venom is a neurotoxin (that is, it affects the nervous system), local treatment is almost useless. The victim should be taken to a physician immediately. For a brown recluse bite, apply an ice pack to the site of the bite to localize the venom and then take the victim immediately to a physician.

The brown recluse is slightly smaller than the black widow, but also has very long legs. Its color varies from light to chocolate brown, and it has six eyes in three pairs (the black widow has eight in two rows) and a dark, violin-shaped marking on the top of the cephalothorax (the region that contains the head and legs). This marking gives the spider one of its common names—the violin- or fiddle-backed spider.

BIOLOGY Black widows are common in protected places like trash piles, stumps, under stones, on weedy road banks, and in water meter boxes. The female is usually found hanging inverted in an irregular tangled web of coarse silk that she uses to trap prey. There is often an egg sac in the web as well. The black widow does occasionally consume her partner after mating with him. In fact, such cannibalism is fairly common among spiders, although not nearly as common as myth would have us believe.

The brown recluse does not like lighted areas and is common in cracks and crevices of old logs, under bark, and beneath flat stones. Inside our home, it takes up residence in places that are generally undisturbed— behind picture frames, beneath sofas, in the back of closets, and so on. The spider spins a flat, irregular web that is used as a resting place rather than a snare. The brown recluse actively hunts its food and leaves the web in search of prey. Brown recluses may be found singly or in "bunches." I once found several hundred in an outbuilding in Spalding County that was used as storage for bottles, cans, and other containers.

IMPACT The black widow is relatively shy and usually does not bite unless provoked. The venom is highly toxic, but fortunately one usually gets only a very small amount with each bite. Small children and elderly individuals are usually the most sensitive. The immediate reaction to a bite ranges from a sharp pain similar to a needle puncture to nothing at all. Local swelling and redness occur, and severe muscle cramps develop within a few minutes. Respiration often becomes labored and spasmodic, and there can be convulsions, nausea and vomiting, light delirium, shock, and insomnia. Brown recluse venom produces a condition called "necrotic arachnoidism." The bite itself may be completely painless or may cause intense pain that lasts 2–8 hours. A small blister forms at the site, and over time the damaged tissue sloughs away, leaving an ulcerous central area with dense scar tissue. The wound heals *very* slowly, and scars as large as a half-dollar have been reported.

CONTROL Removing lumber, rock piles, scrap materials, junk, and old boxes is important in combating spider infestations. Outbuildings suspected of harboring poisonous spiders can be treated with a variety of household sprays. Contact your local county extension office for the most recent recommendations. When applying pesticides, *always* follow the instructions on the label.

Sowbugs and Pillbugs

Invasion of the Bantam Armadillos!

A number of people have contacted me with questions about "tiny armadillo-like" creatures accumulating in large numbers beneath flower pots, rotting boards, stones, and mulch. These tiny animals, which *really do* resemble minuscule armadillos, are sowbugs and pillbugs, and they thrive in moist environments. Though often thought to be insects, these creatures are isopods, and they are more closely related to lobsters, shrimp, and crayfish than to insects.

Sowbugs and pillbugs look like tiny armadillos.

SCIENTIFIC NAME Order Isopoda

IDENTIFICATION Pillbugs and sowbugs are brownish to slate gray, about ¼ to ½ inch long, with convex, slightly elongate bodies covered with shieldlike plates — just like tiny armadillos. They have seven pairs of legs (insects have three pairs) and two pairs of antennae (insects have one), only one of which is easily visible. Sowbugs have two tail-like extensions at the end of the body. Pillbugs lack these extensions, and when disturbed can roll up into a tight ball (like armadillos). This behavior has given them the nicknames "roly-polies" and "pillbugs."

BIOLOGY Mating occurs throughout the year, but mostly in the spring. Females carry their eggs (from seven to two hundred) in a little ventral pouch. The young remain in this pouch for several weeks, until they are able to fend for themselves. There may be one or two generations a year, and individuals can live up to 3 years. Both sowbugs and pillbugs are scavengers, feeding on decaying organic matter and occasionally on young plants and their roots. They prefer areas of high moisture and usually remain hidden beneath solid objects during the day, grouping together to reduce water loss.

Pillbugs often hide under flowerpots.

IMPACT Though damage to plants is seldom significant, the presence of these creatures can be both annoying and unsettling. They may become pests in and around homes where the proper environment exists. They are also common beneath grass clippings, trash, flower bed mulch, and pet droppings. Homeowners become concerned when they find sowbugs in crawl spaces and basements, and the little animals sometimes even invade the first floor. Common entryways are gaps in concrete blocks and the bases of sliding glass doors. Finding them indoors usually indicates a large breeding population outside, near the foundation. Sowbugs and pillbugs do not survive inside more than a few days unless very damp conditions exist.

CONTROL Because these little beasts require lots of moisture, the best way to minimize their numbers indoors is to reduce moisture and hiding places near the foundation. *Any* standing water or situations that cause standing water near the foundation should be addressed.

- Remove heavy mulch, grass clippings, boards, stones, and similar items from the foundation, basement windows, doors, and other possible places of entry.
- Ventilate crawl spaces and basements to reduce moisture, and seal any cracks in the foundation.
- Indoors, use dehumidifiers and fans to dry out damp rooms.

Insecticides inside the home are of little value, but they may be effective in reducing the number of isopods coming inside if sprayed around crawl space entrances, doors and windows, foundation vents, and utility openings. Various common household insecticides are effective.

Photo Credits

ii   Scott Bauer, USDA ARS, www.insectimages.org

13   Susan Ellis, www.insectimages.org

14   Frank Hale, Department of Entomology and Plant Pathology, University of Tennessee, Knoxville

15   Joseph Berger, www.insectimages.org

16   Joseph Berger, www.insectimages.org

19   Robert L. Anderson, USDA Forest Service, www.insectimages.org

21   North Carolina State University

22   North Carolina State University

25   Gerald J. Lenhard, www.insectimages.org

27   USDA APHIS PPQ Archives, USDA APHIS, www.insectimages.org

28   USDA APHIS PPQ Archives, USDA APHIS, www.insectimages.org

29   USDA APHIS PPQ Archives, USDA APHIS, www.insectimages.org

31   Clemson University — USDA Cooperative Extension Slide Series, www.insectimages.org

35   Frank Hale, Department of Entomology and Plant Pathology, University of Tennessee, Knoxville

36   Jerry A. Payne, USDA ARS, www.insectimages.org

37   Clemson University — USDA Cooperative Extension Slide Series, www.insectimages.org

41   Jerry A. Payne, USDA ARS, www.insectimages.org

43   Edward L. Manigault, Clemson University Donated Collection, www.insectimages.org

46   Jerry A. Payne, USDA Agricultural Research Service, www.insectimages.org

47   North Carolina State University

49   Copyright © 2004 David E. Reed

50   Walton Harris

53   Frank Hale, Department of Entomology and Plant Pathology, University of Tennessee, Knoxville

56   Scott Bauer, USDA ARS, www.insectimages.org

59   Frank Hale, Department of Entomology and Plant Pathology, University of Tennessee, Knoxville

60   Scott Bauer, USDA ARS, www.insectimages.org

63   Lacy L. Hyche, Auburn University, www.insectimages.org

65   Clemson University—USDA Cooperative Extension Slide Series, www.insectimages.org

69   Clemson University—USDA Cooperative Extension Slide Series, www.insectimages.org

70   Frank Hale, Department of Entomology and Plant Pathology, University of Tennessee, Knoxville

73   Ronald F. Billings, Texas Forest Service, www.insectimages.org

75   Tom Coleman, University of Kentucky, www.insectimages.org

77   Clemson University—USDA Cooperative Extension Slide Series, www.insectimages.org

81   Frank Hale, Department of Entomology and Plant Pathology, University of Tennessee, Knoxville

83   Clemson University—USDA Cooperative Extension Slide Series, www.insectimages.org

86   Clemson University—USDA Cooperative Extension Slide Series, www.insectimages.org

87   Frank Hale, Department of Entomology and Plant Pathology, University of Tennessee, Knoxville

89   North Carolina State University

91   Clemson University—USDA Cooperative Extension Slide Series, www.insectimages.org

93   Frank Hale, Department of Entomology and Plant Pathology, University of Tennessee, Knoxville

96   North Carolina State University

97   North Carolina State University

98   Jack Kelly Clark, University of California

99   Frank Hale, Department of Entomology and Plant Pathology, University of Tennessee, Knoxville

102   Gerald J. Lenhard, www.insectimages.org

105   Susan Ellis, www.insectimages.org

109   Clemson University — USDA Cooperative Extension Slide Series, www.insectimages.org

110   Clemson University — USDA Cooperative Extension Slide Series, www.insectimages.org

111   Jim Occi, BugPics, www.insectimages.org

116   Whitney Cranshaw, Colorado State University, www.insectimages.org

118   North Carolina State University

119   Frank Hale, Department of Entomology and Plant Pathology, University of Tennessee, Knoxville

120   Ronald F. Billings, Texas Forest Service, www.insectimages.org

122   Jim Howell

123   Steven Kunkle

125   Hansell F. Cross, Georgia State University, www.insectimages.org

129   Jim Kalisch, Department of Entomology, University of Nebraska, Lincoln

132   North Carolina State University

135   Photo © Alex Wild

139   Photo © Alex Wild

140   Copyright © 2004 Tom Murray

141   Jeff Hahn, University of Minnesota.

145   Clemson University — USDA Cooperative Extension Slide Series, www.insectimages.org

147   Clemson University — USDA Cooperative Extension Slide Series, www.insectimages.org

150   Clemson University — USDA Cooperative Extension Slide Series, www.insectimages.org

153   Cereal Research Centre, AAFC

155   Clemson University — USDA Cooperative Extension Slide Series, www.insectimages.org

159   Clemson University — USDA Cooperative Extension Slide Series, www.insectimages.org

161   Clemson University — USDA Cooperative Extension Slide Series, www.insectimages.org

165   Cereal Research Centre, AAFC

166   Clemson University — USDA Cooperative Extension Slide Series, www.insectimages.org

170   Maria Eisner, Cornell University

173   Vincent S. Smith

177   Clemson University — USDA Cooperative Extension Slide Series, www.insectimages.org

181   Clemson University — USDA Cooperative Extension Slide Series, www.insectimages.org

184   Stephen Armour

185   Andy Purviance, www.purviance.com

187   Clemson University — USDA Cooperative Extension Slide Series, www.insectimages.org

193   Joseph Berger, www.insectimages.org

195   BelKraft International; visit www.belkraft.com/news.htm

199   Joseph Berger, www.insectimages.org

201   Clemson University — USDA Cooperative Extension Slide Series, www.insectimages.org

202   Frank Hale, Department of Entomology and Plant Pathology, University of Tennessee, Knoxville

205   Andy Purviance, www.purviance.com

206   Jim Howell

Index

abdomen, 4

Acari, 117, 126, 128, 195

Achaearanea tepidariorum (C. L. Koch), 198

Acrididae, 108

Actias luna (Linnaeus), 76

Aedes albopictus (Skuse), 106

Aleyrodidae, 96

allergies, 195

Amblyomma americanum (Linnaeus), 128

American cockroach, 144

American house spider, 198–200

anaphylactic reaction, 29

anaphylaxis, 54

Anisoptera, 12

Anobiidae, 162

ant: black carpenter ant, 32; carpenter ant, 31–33; fire ant, 27–30

antenna, 4

ant lion, 15

aphid, 59–62

Apidae, 34

Apis mellifera Linnaeus, 34

aposematic, 109

Arachnida, 3, 5, 7, 120

Araneae, 198

Arctiidae, 68

Argiope aurantia Lucas, 120

Argiopidae, 120

Arilus cristatus Linnaeus, 94

Arthropoda, 3

Asian lady beetle, 57

Asian tiger mosquito, 105–7

assassin bug, 94

Bacillus thuringiensis, 64, 69

bagworm, 63–64

bald-faced hornet, 43–45

barklice, 153

batbug, 132–34

bedbug, 132–34

bee: bumble bee, 37–39; carpenter bee, 40–42; honey bee, 34–36

beetle: carpet beetle, 155–57; cigarette beetle, 161–63; green June beetle, 99, 100; Japanese beetle, 100; ladybug, 56–58; saw-toothed grain beetle, 164–65

Big Dipper firefly, 103

black-and-yellow mud dauber, 50–51

black carpenter ant, 32

Black Death, 169

black widow, 51, 201–4
Blatta orientalis (Linnaeus), 151
Blattaria, 144, 148, 151
Blattella germanica (Linnaeus), 148
Blattellidae, 147
Blattidae, 144, 151
blowfly, 23
blue bottle fly, 22
blue mud dauber, 50, 51
Boisea trivittatus (Say), 77
Bombidae, 38
Bombus sp., 38
booklouse, 153–54
boxelder bug, 77–79
brown recluse, 201–4
bubonic plague, 169
bumble bee, 37–39

Calliphora vomitoria (L.), 22
Calliphoridae, 22, 142
camel cricket, 181–83
Camponotus sp., 32
Carolina mantid, 18
carpenter ant, 31–33
carpenter bee, 40–42
carpet beetle, 155–57
case-making clothes moth, 167
caterpillar: fall webworm, 68–69;
    hickory horned devil, 73–74; tent
    caterpillar, 65–67; yellow-necked
    caterpillar, 70–72

cat flea, 169
centipede, 122–24
cephalothorax, 7
cerci, 184
Cercopidae, 91
Ceuthophilus spp., 181
chafer, 100
Chagas' disease, 94
Chalybion californicum (Saussure), 50
chelicerae, 7
chigger, 125–27
Chilopoda, 5, 122
Chinese mantid, 18
cicada, 111–13
cicada killer, 24–26
Cicadidae, 111
cigarette beetle, 161–63
Cimex adjunctus Barber, 132
Cimex lectularis (Linnaeus), 132
Cimicidae, 132
Citheronia regalis (Fabricius), 73
citrus whitefly, 96–98
clothes moth, 166–68
cluster fly, 141–43
Coccinellidae, 56
cockroach, 144–46; American cock-
    roach, 144; German cockroach,
    147–49; Oriental cockroach, 150–52;
    smoky brown cockroach, 144–45
Coleoptera, 56, 100, 103, 156, 162, 164
common house spider, 198–200

complete metamorphosis, 3, 7

cootie, 173

Coptotermes formosanus (Shiraki), 176

cornicle, 60

Cotinus nitida (Linnaeus), 100

cricket, camel, 181–83

Crustacea, 5

Cryptotermes brevis (Walker), 176

Ctenocephalides canis (Curtis), 169

Ctenocephalides felis (Bouche), 169

Ctenolepisma sp., 187

Culicidae, 106

daddy-longlegs, 192–94

damselfly, 12–14

Datana ministra (Drury), 71

Dermacentor variabilis (Say), 128

Dermaptera, 184

Dermatophagoides sp., 195

Dermestidae, 156

Dialeurodes citri (Ashmead), 96

Diaphania nitidalis (Stoll), 86

Diaspididae, 80

Diplopoda, 5, 122

Diptera, 22, 106, 136, 138, 142

dog-day cicada, 111–13

dog flea, 169

Dolichovespula maculata Linnaeus, 44

doodlebug, 15–17

dragonfly, 12–14

Drosophila sp., 138

Drosophilidae, 138

dust mite, 195–97

earwig, 184–86

Eastern subterranean termite, 176

elytra, 7, 57

euonymus scales, 80–82

fall webworm, 68–69

family, 3

Far Side, The (Larson), 2

femur, 4

fire ant, 27–30

firebrat, 187–89

firefly, 102–4

flea, 169–72

fly: blowfly, 23; blue bottle fly, 22; citrus whitefly, 96–98; cluster fly, 141–43; damselfly, 12–14; dragonfly, 12–14; firefly, 102–4; fruit fly, 138–40; green bottle fly, 22; moth fly, 135–37

Forficulidae, 184

Formicidae, 28, 32

Formosan subterranean termite, 176

frass, 70

fruit fly, 138–40

genus, 3

German cockroach, 147–49

golden garden spider, 119–21

gradual metamorphosis, 3
grasshopper, lubber, 108–10
green bottle fly, 22
green June beetle, 99, 100
grub worm, 99–101
Gryllacrididae, 181
guinea wasp, 47

harvestmen, 192
hawk moth, 84
head louse, 173–75
hemimetabolous, 3, 7
Hemiptera, 77, 89, 93
Hexapoda, 3
hickory horned devil, 73–74
holometabolous, 3, 7
Homoptera, 59, 80, 91, 96, 111
honey bee, 34–36
honeydew, 59, 61
hornet, 43–45
hornworm, 83–85
house spider, 198–200
Hymenoptera: Apidae, 34; Bombidae, 38; cicada killer, 24; organ pipe mud dauber, 50; paper wasp, 52; *Polistes*, 52; *Sceliphron caementarium* (Drury), 50; *Solenopsis invicta* Buren, 28; Vespidae, 44; *Vespula maculifrons* (Buysson), 46; *Vespula squamosa* (Drury), 46; yellowjacket, 46
Hyphantria cunea (Drury), 68

Indian meal moth, 158–60
instar, 3, 7
Isoptera, 176
Ixodes scapularis Say, 128
Ixodidae, 128

Japanese beetle, 100
jarfly, 111

Kalotermitidae, 176
kingdom, 3

lace bug, 89–90
La Crosse encephalitis, 107
ladybug, 56–58
Lampyridae, 103
Larson, Gary, 138
larva, 8
Lasiocampidae, 65
Lasioderma serricorne (Fabricius), 162
Latrodectus sp., 202
Lepidoptera: Arctiidae, 68; bagworm, 63; case-making clothes moth, 167; *Citheronia regalis* (Fabricius), 73; *Diaphania nitidalis* (Stoll), 86; fall webworm, 68; hornworm, 83; *Hyphantria cunea* (Drury), 68; Indian meal moth, 158; Lasiocampidae, 63; *Malacosoma americanum* (Fabricius), 65; *Manduca quinquemaculata* (Haworth), 83; *Melittia cucurbitae* (Harris), 158; pickleworm, 86;

Plodia interpunctella (Hubner), 158; Psychidae, 63; Pyralidae, 86, 158; royal walnut moth, 73; Saturniidae, 73, 76; Sesiidae, 86; Sphingidae, 83; squash vine borer, 86; tent caterpillar, 65; *Thyridopteryx ephemeraeformis* (Haworth), 63; *Tinea pellionella*, 167; Tineidae, 167; *Tineola bisselliella*, 167; webbing clothes moth, 167

Lepisma saccharina Linnaeus, 187

Lepismatidae, 187

lice, head, 173–75

lightningbug, 102–4

locust, 111

louse, head, 173–75

Loxosceles reclusa Gertsch and Mulaik, 202

Loxoscelidae, 202

lubber grasshopper, 108–10

luna moth, 75–76

maggot, 21–23

Malacosoma americanum (Fabricius), 63

Manduca quinquemaculata (Haworth), 83

Mantidae, 18

mantis, 18–20

Mantoidea, 18

May beetle, 100

Melittia cucurbitae (Harris), 86

metamorphosis, 8

millipede, 122–24

mite, 3, 5, 35–36, 57, 192, 201; dust mite, 195–97; red harvest mite, 125, 126; spider mite, 116–18

mosquito, 105–7

moth: bagworm moth, 63; clothes moth, 166–68; hawk moth, 84; Indian meal moth, 158–60; luna moth, 75–76; royal walnut moth, 74. *See also* caterpillar

moth fly, 135–37

mud dauber, 49–51

Myrmeleontidae, 15

Neuroptera, 15

nits, 173

northern black widow, 202

Notodontidae, 71

nymph, 8

Odonata, 12

ootheca, 8

Opiliones, 192

order, 3

organ pipe mud dauber, 50

Oriental cockroach, 150–52

Orthoptera, 108, 181

Oryzaephilus surinamensis (Linnaeus), 165

ovipositor, 182

palmetto bug, 144, 145
paper wasp, 52–55
parasites, 3
parthenogenesis, 60, 153
Pediculidae, 173
Pediculus humanus capitis De Geer, 173
periodical cicada, 112
Periplaneta americana (Linnaeus), 144
Periplaneta fuliginosa (Serville), 144
pesticides, 6
Phaenicia sericata (Meigen), 22
Phalangidae, 192
Photinus pyralis (Linnaeus), 103
Phthiraptera, 173
Phyllophaga sp., 100
phylum, 3
phytophages, 3
pickleworm, 86–88
pillbug, 4, 205–7
Plodia interpunctella (Hubner), 158
Polistes, 52
Pollenia rudis (Fabricius), 142
Popillia japonica Newman, 100
praying mantis, 18–20
predaceous, 8
predators, 3
pronotum, 4, 8
Prosapia bicinta (Say), 91
Psocidae, 153
Psocoptera, 153
Psychidae, 63

Psychoda sp., 135
Psychodidae, 135
Pulicidae, 169
pupation, 8
Pyralidae, 86, 158
Pyroglyphidae, 196

redbug, 125
Reduviidae, 94
Reticulitermes flavipes (Kollar), 176
Rhinotermitidae, 176
Rhopalida, 77
Romalea guttata (Houttuyn), 108
royal walnut moth, 73

saprophytic, 8
Saturniidae, 73, 76
saw-toothed grain beetle, 164–65
Scarabeidae, 100
Sceliphron caementarium (Drury), 50
semiomnivorous, 156
serrate (antennae), 162
Sesiidae, 86
setae, 8
Silvanidae, 164
silverfish, 187–89
Siphonaptera, 169
smoky brown cockroach, 144–45
snake doctor, 12
Solenopsis invicta Buren, 28
sooty mold, 59

southern black widow, 202

sowbug, 4, 205–7

species, 3

Sphecidae, 24, 50

Sphecius speciosus (Drury), 24

Sphingidae, 83

spider, 3, 5, 7, 8; black widow, 51, 201–4; brown recluse, 201–4; enemies, 50, 51, 71, 122; golden garden spider, 119–21; house spider, 198–200

spider mite, 116–18

spiracle, 4, 8

spittlebug, 91–92

squash vine borer, 86–88

stabilimentum, 8

Stagmomantis carolina (Johannson), 18

stings, treatment for, 54

stylostomes, 127

tarsus, 4, 8

Tenodera aridifolia sinensis Saussure, 18

tent caterpillar, 65–67

termite, 176–80

Tetranychidae, 117

Theridiidae, 198, 202

Thermobia domestica (Packard), 187

thorax, 4

Thyridopteryx ephemeraeformis (Haworth), 63

Thysanura, 187

tibia, 4, 8

Tibicen spp., 111

tick, 128–30

Tinea bisselliella, 167

Tinea pellionella, 167

Tineidae, 167

Tingidae, 89

tracheae, 8

tracheal mite, 36

Trombicula alfreddugesi (Oudemans), 126

Trombiculidae, 125

trypanosomiasis, 94

Trypoxylon sp., 50

two-lined spittlebug, 91

Unaspis euonymi (Comstock), 80

varroa mite, 36

Vespidae, 44, 46, 52

Vespula maculifrons (Buysson), 46

Vespula squamosa (Drury), 46

vine borer, 86–88

wasp: hornet, 43–45; mud dauber, 49–51; paper wasp, 52–55; yellow-jacket, 46–48

water bug, 151

webbing clothes moth, 167

webworm, fall, 68–69

West Indian powderpost termite, 176

wheel bug, 93–95

whitefly, 96–98

white grub, 99–101

Xylocopa virginica Linnaeus, 40

Xylocopidae, 40

yellow fever mosquito, 106

yellowjacket, 46–48

yellow-necked caterpillar, 70–72

Yersinia pestis, 169

Zygoptera, 12